How to Build a Career in the New Economy

How to Build a Career in the New Economy

A Guide for Minorities and Women

By
Anthony Stith

Warwick Publishing
Toronto   Los Angeles
www.warwickgp.com

Also by Anthony Stith:
Breaking the Glass Ceiling: Sexism and Racism in Corporate America—The Myths, the Realities and the Solutions
(Warwick Publishing, 1998)

We acknowledge the financial support of the Government of Canada through the Book Publishing Industry Development Program for our publishing activities.

ISBN: 1-894020-48-0

Published by Warwick Publishing Inc.
162 John Street, Suite 300, Toronto, Ontario, Canada M5V 2E5

Cover design: Heidi Gemmill
Editorial Services: Melinda Tate

Printed and bound in Canada.

Table of Contents

- *Responsibility Must Be Accompanied by Authority*
- *We Must Not Only Prepare for the Future, We Must Embrace It*
- *Make Education a Lifelong Occupation*
- *Show Appreciation to Others*
- *A Positive Image*
- *You Can't Please Everyone So Don't Try*
- *Hire Qualified Employees*
- *Planning and Organization*
- *Treat Each Person as an Individual*
- *Empower Yourself*
- *The Secrets of Success*

Resources *235*

References *241*

Introduction

THIRTY years ago, there was no need for a career guide specifically designed for minorities and women. That's because minorities and women didn't have careers. For African Americans, Hispanics, and other minorities, finding a job that paid a decent wage was the most they could hope for. And while the term "career girl" was not unknown, the key word was "girl." Women were not seen as serious contenders for upper-level positions in the corporate world. Those who dared to challenge these attitudes faced immense, often insurmountable barriers.

But even in those days, minorities and women were realizing that they did not have to sit back and accept this situation. Due to the effort of many courageous individuals and organizations, attitudes and laws have changed. The idea of women and minorities building careers for themselves is no longer futile. In fact, things have gotten so much better in the working world for minorities and women that you might ask why they need their own career guide today.

The sad fact is, despite the great gains that have been made, racism and sexism persist. These evils may not be as obvious or visible as they once were (though sometimes they still are), but in many corporations, institutions, and individuals, they lurk beneath the surface. In recent years, a number of large companies, such as the

Denny's restaurant chain, Boeing and United Parcel Service have had to deal with accusations of racial discrimination in the last few years. Others have had to pay damages in lawsuits for sexual harassment.

Statistics show the gaps, particularly as minority and women employees attempt to move up the corporate ladder. A survey by the American Management Association in 1998 showed that though more women are moving into policy-making positions in the private sector, female managers' salaries lagged behind those of their male colleagues by an average of 63 percent (quoted in *Sales & Marketing Management*, Nov./98, p. 98). A series of studies by Catalyst in the mid-1990s showed that in the private sector, for every dollar white male managers earn, women of color earn 57 cents on average, white women managers earn 59 cents, and men-of-color managers earn 75 cents (quoted in *Business Week,* Aug. 10/98).

Furthermore, the last few years have seen a backlash against measures aimed at removing these inequities. In the United States, many states have struck down affirmative action laws. In Canada in 1998, the federal government was engaged in a court battle to avoid following its own "equal pay for work of equal value" rules.

In addition to these challenges, minorities and women, like everybody else, must adapt to the realities of the New Economy. Rapid technological change and globalization have eliminated many jobs. The time when dependable employees were virtually guaranteed a lifetime position in their companies is over.

But the New Economy has also brought new opportunities and new, exciting, well-paying jobs. This is especially important for minorities and women. New products and services develop so rapidly that there is no time to develop prejudices about who should be allowed to work where. Now more than ever, minorities and women have the chance to build careers that are financially and emotionally satisfying.

Taking advantage of all the career opportunities presented by the New Economy requires getting rid of old assumptions. Minorities and women are possibly more apt than others to fall prey to these old beliefs. In the past, being hard working and well-educated were their only keys to gaining the limited types of employment open to them. But these traits no longer have the impact they once did. Hard work alone will not get or keep a job. Degrees, diplomas and certificates do not guarantee success in the real working world. While hard work and education are still important elements in building careers, there are many other factors you need to be aware of.

Above all, building a career requires active planning. This book will show you how. It is your map for reaching your career goals. It will help you discover the right career for you. You'll find out how to break through the barriers that prevent minorities and women from reaching their full career potential. You'll learn techniques for dealing with day-to-day challenges, like working for difficult bosses. You'll get numerous tips and tricks for landing promotions. And you'll see how to maintain your career success once you find it.

Success in our careers is closely tied to our success in life. This is why minorities and women have worked so hard to get rid of the discrimination that has prevented them from participating fully in the working world. We all know it is not enough to work merely to provide the basics of life. Humans need work that means more than just a steady paycheck. We need the feeling of accomplishment that work can bring. We need to feel we are making a contribution to society. We need to have our contribution acknowledged. This is why building a career through careful planning, constant learning, and perseverance is so important.

As I will show in chapter 1, there is a big difference between a job and a career. A job just pays your rent. A well-planned career can enhance your whole life. Carefully devising your career path is one of the best things you can do for yourself. This book is a great place to start.

Chapter 1

Creating a Successful Career

Before everything else, getting ready is the secret of success.

—HENRY FORD

BEFORE you can seek success in a career you must understand some important principles. They determine your level of success or failure long before your first day at work.

Unfortunately, most African Americans, other minorities and women fail to grasp these principles. They tend to base their career choices solely on how much money they will earn when they are hired. This kind of thinking is a holdover from the days when members of these groups had very few career options. At one time, the only employment they could expect to find was low paid and boring. As a result, their view of the working world tended to be negative. Their only measurement of a "good job" was how much it paid.

Today, minorities and women have many more career options. But they do not seem to have adjusted their attitudes toward paid work. This is one of the reasons why most minorities and women fail to find fulfillment, financial security, and happiness in their careers.

We need to become aware of these conditioned responses and replace them with new approaches. If you incorporate the five principles listed below into your life, you will find success and fulfillment. It requires a commitment to follow these principles, but their results far outweigh the effort it takes to apply them.

FIVE PRINCIPLES THAT MAKE CAREERS SUCCESSFUL

1. Know the Difference between a Career and a Job

African Americans, minorities and women must stop seeking "jobs." Instead of seeking jobs, they should be seeking careers.

There is a world of difference between having a job and having a career. A job is something we go to because we need money to pay bills. When we accept a job, it is for the sole purpose of obtaining money. The difference between jobs and careers becomes evident when we ask ourselves if the money provided by our jobs creates self-worth and happiness. How much money does it take to make us feel fulfilled? Without considering your income, does your job make you feel good? Are you proud of what you do to earn your income? Does it allow you to sleep comfortably at night?

The dictionary defines "job" as *an action requiring some exertion; a task, an undertaking. An activity performed in exchange for payment; especially, performed regularly as one's trade, occupation, or profession.*

The dictionary defines "career" as *a chosen pursuit; a profession or occupation. The general course or progression of one's life, especially one's profession. A path or course. A rapid course or swift progression, speed. The moment of highest pitch or peak activity. To move or run at full speed; go headlong; rush.*

As you can see, the definitions of the words "career" and "job" are different. The reasons why and the manner in which we perform them are based on different motives and objectives. The dictionary uses words and phrases such as, "exertion," "task," "undertaking" and "exchange for payment" to describe a job. None of these words show a job is pleasurable or something to look forward to doing.

The dictionary uses words and phrases such as "chosen pursuit," "progression of one's life," "moments of highest pitch or peak activity" to define a career. These words and phrases describe something we enjoy and look forward to every day. My definition of career is *something we desire to make a significant part of our lives. It provides feelings of satisfaction and enjoyment during the process of performing it. The activities in our careers give us something to look forward to each day. They provide feelings of self-worth, purpose, and a mission in life.*

A true career is something we would miss if we were unable to do it. It is something we willingly and freely devote one hundred and ten percent of our time and energy to. A career provides personal growth, opportunities, and financial rewards. It's something we are passionate about.

My definition of a job is *what we do out of necessity to earn a living to provide food, shelter and security. A job is anything you take to earn a living regardless of personal satisfaction. A job is what you do to earn money. Earning money is the only reason you work. A job is something you would leave in a flash if someone was willing to pay you a few dollars more.*

A job is something we resent doing. It makes us stressful, unhappy, and taxes our mental and physical health. It is something we spend our working and social hours complaining about. The constant whining about our jobs alienates us from friends and family. It often reaches the point where no one wants to associate with us for fear of having to listen to us talk about our horrible jobs.

We should not take this to mean that all jobs are difficult and all careers easy. We can have a job that is easy and a career that is demanding. The differences are the rewards we receive from them. When a job is demanding and difficult, it is perceived as a frustrating, non-enjoyable chore. When we have a job, staying motivated is difficult, and completing undesirable tasks is a strain. Our weekly paycheck or fears of being fired are our motivating factors. Since we are not getting paid or fired at the time we are doing these onerous tasks, our motivation is likely to be low or nonexistent.

People with jobs rely on a strong work ethic alone to complete the difficult, undesirable tasks their work entails. When our work ethic is all that keeps us going, problems soon develop. We soon find ourselves in a constant state of turmoil. We perform our set tasks because we feel duty-bound to do so and are paid for doing them. At the same time, we dread work because we lack interest in it and the desire to perform it. There is a constant struggle between our emotions and values. The result is only stress, discomfort, and unhappiness.

It's a myth to believe a strong work ethic alone is enough to sustain us over long periods without love for what we do. Relying on a strong work ethic without a passion for what we do is often our greatest source of frustration.

The disparity between our wish to fulfill our duties and our desire to do them eventually makes our jobs unbearable, causing our performance to deteriorate. This results in our loss of self confidence and feelings of worthlessness. Only money binds us to our jobs. This happens to even the best employees who maintain jobs instead of building careers.

We develop a different attitude when we have careers. When we have a career, we view difficult tasks as challenges and barriers we will overcome. With a career, our objectives and desired results highly motivate us.

Successful people have passion for their careers. This passion sustains them during difficult times. It allows them to see negative situations as obstacles they are willing to overcome. Careers give us instant gratification as we perform our duties. Selecting the right career propels us toward success and happiness.

Understanding the difference between a job and career is the first step toward achieving success.

2. Actively Plan Your Career

Too many of us begin our employment search with the newspaper classified section. We look for anything that is available. There are three problems with this:

First, it means we are just looking for a job instead of a career. For reasons explained above, this is a recipe for disaster.

The second problem is, using the newspaper classified section, or chance or luck as our primary sources for obtaining and developing a career are all ways of leaving it to outside circumstances to control our destiny. When we do this, we are rendering ourselves powerless.

Instead, we must take charge of our lives. As Benjamin Disraeli said, "Man is not the creature of circumstances, circumstances are the creatures of man." We must not see ourselves as victims of events that are out of our control. It is our responsibility and obligation to *create* the circumstances for our career success.

A third problem with the want-ad approach is that it doesn't allow us to predetermine the career of our choice. When we fail to expend the time and energy to develop a career plan, we end up accepting any jobs that become available. Poor financial situations often mandate this. But when we do this, we create the foundation for our own failure. When we take any job we can find because we failed to plan our careers, we can end up locked into undesirable work for life. This is a frightening and dismal thought.

The first step in avoiding these problems is to make a conscious career choice. Unfortunately, our educational system does not provide proper career guidance for most students. Too many people finish high school or college with little or no idea of the career they will pursue. With proper career counselling they could have assessed their talents, skills and interests and then received a range of suitable career options to explore.

Instead, lacking proper guidance, many individuals select professions that are not suitable for them. They may base their decisions on what's available or convenient at the time they are looking for work. They may choose to follow what their relatives or friends do for a living. Either way, this is a hit and miss process. The likelihood of ending up doing work that enhances their lives is pretty slim.

Excellent career choices are ones that involve activities you love. I cannot overstate the importance of selecting a career you enjoy. Doing what you love to do is more than just a career. It's a joy. It creates a passion for living. It allows you to live life to the fullest. Even more important, when you near the end of your life, you can look back with few regrets. You won't feel life passed you by without doing the things you wished and dreamed you had done. Finding the right career is one of the greatest gifts life has to offer.

You are probably asking, how can I decide what career will make me happy before I experience it? The answer is not complicated. Just try to decide what you enjoy doing, what your abilities and talents are, and what gives you self-satisfaction.

The first step is to determine your interests. Many of us never discover what really interests us because we unconsciously impose limits on ourselves. By the time we reach adulthood, we've established certain habits and ways of thinking. We tend to move within a set social circle. We mock the unknown and discredit new ideas and experiences. We shy away from or ignore people who are different from us. We never explore the endless possibilities life offers. We stay within our comfort zone, among the things we are familiar with.

When we make our move into the working world, we emulate our family members and friends. We think if they like it, we should too. Even when we don't enjoy what these individuals do, they often influence our decisions. We become what they are and not who we are. We try to please others instead of ourselves.

We are bombarded with prejudices, frustrations and negative experiences from our families, friends and environment. We constantly hear how African Americans, minorities and women cannot find good careers, how unfairly they are treated in the working world. This negative thinking can set us up for failure even before we start our careers. It creates a fear of having a career. This fear paralyzes us. We never establish careers or we fail in our careers because we believed we would fail even before we started.

Many of us never find work that interests us because we allow all these outside influences to determine what we do, rather than discover what is best for us. Breaking out of this pattern requires a conscious effort. It can be frightening to move away from our comfort zone. We may worry about failing or making fools of ourselves if we try something new. We may fear being rejected if we try to approach people outside of our social class or ethnic background. Mastering such fears and worries is the first step in creating a more fulfilling life for yourself. Focus on all the positive aspects of this process, not on the negative things that might occur. In any case, if you are not happy in your present situation, what have you got to lose?

Remember that opportunities for women and minorities have greatly expanded — women can be mechanics; African Americans can be CEOs. Don't let the fears and prejudices of others keep you from exploring new avenues. Learn from others' negative experiences but don't let them hold you back.

Another reason you need to try new things is because there are so many new things to try. The high technology revolution creates new positions and work titles all the time. How about becoming a webmaster or a multimedia content developer? Do you even know what these people do? If you don't, maybe you should find out — you may discover the career of your dreams!

There are many ways of finding out what kind of work might interest you. If you are still in school, visit your guidance counselor or career center. Ask to take aptitude tests. There are a number of them out there that will help you see where your skills lie. The results may surprise you. You may even learn about occupations you never knew existed. If your school doesn't offer these services, try a government employment office. You can also pay for professional career counseling, but it can be quite costly.

Of little or no cost and of perhaps greater benefit, is to devise your own program of discovery. It simply involves getting out there, trying new things and meeting new people. Ask positive and successful individuals about their professions, their likes and dislikes. Maintain an open mind about careers and occupations that are new and different. Read about people, what they do, where they go, and their experiences. Hobbies, school, volunteer work, social and business relationships and organizations, libraries, TV, radio and church contacts can reveal career possibilities. The key is to expose yourself to as many experiences as possible. See how these activities make you feel about yourself.

Selecting the right career requires that you take the time to know yourself. If you limit your experiences and exposure to what mere circumstance has presented to you during your lifetime, you will never know for sure what you are capable of. Once you know your interests and have explored career opportunities you can make an informed choice about what type of career to pursue.

In fact, you'll probably come up with a number of career options that interest you. You may see it as a problem to figure out which option in particular to focus on. This is not really a problem, for another important aspect of a successful working life is to always have multiple options.

You do have a real problem if you end up with only one option. You need alternatives should your primary career plans fail to materialize. For instance, small numbers of blacks have successful and highly visible careers in entertainment and professional sports. This has caused the black population to express unrealistic interest in these careers. People tend to forget that only a small segment of the population will achieve success in the sports and entertainment fields. Therefore, it is unwise to single-mindedly pursue a career as a basketball player or professional musician. If the career never materializes or ends prematurely due to injury or changes in the public's tastes, there is nothing to fall back on. This is why we must have alternative career options.

Alternative career options can also sustain us until we are ready to return to our first career choice. In any area of endeavor, circumstances can end our careers. These circumstances can be beyond your control. New technological advances can make career and professions obsolete. Understanding that sometimes our first career choice may not be possible is important.

Having options provides security and confidence. They make it easier to succeed in our first career choice. Security and confidence overcome our fear of failure, the chief cause of disasters in our careers. We also may simply wish to change careers later on. A career change in later life can be invigorating, so it's good to have a number of options to explore.

Deciding which option to explore first may be a challenge. Your present financial situation may have a heavy influence on your decision, but never make the fatal mistake of thinking of payment solely in financial terms. Think of payment as gaining experience, contacts, references, future career offers. Seek out knowledgeable people in the career you are pursuing. Use them as mentors and role models. Learn from their successes and failures. Contact organizations and businesses that relate to your career. Seek information to gain insight into your career, make contacts and friends. Volunteer your time to gain experience and exposure in your career. These activities open doors and create opportunities.

Once you select your career(s), immediately work toward establishing yourself in them. This means working out a career plan. Successful people planned their careers long before they started their first day of work. Unsuccessful people relied on newspaper classified ads, chance, luck, friends and families for jobs. Learn to create opportunities for yourself by making contacts, promoting yourself and gaining valuable experience in advance.

Grammar or high school is the ideal time to start developing career goals. Parents should encourage their children to have some idea of the career they want before they graduate from high school. This choice does not have to be locked in stone and can change later, but it helps students to start gearing themselves toward a career. We can also make new career plans when we are older. You may be working at a dead-end job or have just lost interest. It is never too late to start developing a career. The only limits in your career are the limits you place on yourself.

Devising a Career Plan

Once you have some idea about which career is best for you, you must work out the practical details of how to attain it. Your answers to the following questions will give you the framework for your plan:

1. What is your career goal?
2. What is your time frame for reaching your goal?
3. Do you have what it takes to be successful in your career?

Establish Your Career Goal(s). It is not enough to know what type of career we want. We must also establish goals for our careers. The sum of our individual goals is the foundation of our success in our careers. Establishing goals for our career is just as important as selecting the right career. Without goals our career lacks direction and purpose. Our self-esteem soars when we establish career goals that become our life's mission. They are an important part of who we are. They give us joy, satisfaction and purpose.

Our career goals do not come alive or have meaning for us until we write them down. Putting our career goals in writing transforms them from thoughts into reality. They become something we can see, touch and are responsible for. Career goals must be written as brief statements and reviewed daily. Here's an example of a written goal:

> *I want to be president and owner of my company by age 35. My company will specialize in health care for children. It will earn annual profits of 20 million dollars and treat 20,000 children a year. It will be recognized as the industry's leading company in pediatric health care.*

Only when your goals are meaningful to you will you strive for them year after year. They will sustain you in times of difficulty. Your career goal becomes a special part of you that you love and cherish. Goals must be challenging. Overcoming challenges creates feelings of self-worth. Goals must be challenging enough that you must exert yourself, but not to the point where you dread the prospect of trying to overcome them.

Set both long-term and short-term goals. Long-term goals may seem daunting or unattainable — your goal to own your company by age 35 when you're just starting as a 20-year-old office assistant may seem impossible. Breaking it down into a series of short-term, doable steps can keep you from being overwhelmed. For example:

Long-term goal:	To be company president by the time I'm 35.
Short-term goals:	Become supervisor by age 22; department manager by age 25; regional manager by 28 ...

and so on. These short-term goals may be broken down further to whatever level is comfortable for you. As you reach each short-term goal, your feeling of achievement will encourage you to continue.

Establish Time Frames for Your Goals. Establishing time frames for career goals is a critical tool to ensure success. Time frames are gauges to determine your progress. They let you know if you are on the right or wrong track. They are signals to determine what's working and what's not. Time frames require you to take inventory of yourself and others, and to look at what's going on around you. When things are not working, they make you seek new solutions. They force you to ask questions that will help keep you focused on your goals.

Set realistic time frames. Unrealistic time frames set you up for failure or ridicule. If you miss a time frame, don't view it as a failure; it just means either you did not plan properly or you set an unrealistic time frame. Do not be ashamed if you do not meet your goals' time frames, but learn from your mistakes. Use these experiences to help you succeed in your career goals.

Acquire the Skills Needed to be Successful. Education, training and tools are needed to succeed in careers. Some careers are specialized while others require general skills. Make a detailed listing of the skills and training you need to be successful. You may discover the skills and training needed last year are no longer sufficient today.

Once you list the skills and training needed for today's success, rate yourself. Do you have the skills and training to be successful? If you have them, are they more than proficient? Are your training and skills up to date? If you had to leave your employer today, would you be able to compete successfully in the current market in your field? If you cannot answer yes to these questions, you need to update your skills.

Most skills and training are obvious, but some skills critical to the success of your career are not. When we think of skills, we tend to think of practical, measurable things, like having the ability to type

80 words a minute or to repair a photocopier. These skills may be important to achieving your specific goal, but there are other, less obvious skills we all need to master in order to move ahead. In most careers, it is critical to be able to work with others. To be successful we must be counselors, diplomats, teachers and disciplinarians. To be successful we must be able to sell ourselves and our ideas. We must learn to communicate with others socially and professionally. Other qualities such as humor, wit, discipline and the ability to handle stress are critical components of successful careers.

Unfortunately, not many of these skills are taught in school. You must take it upon yourself to acquire these skills and improve on them. You can do this by observing successful people. You've probably seen how some people progress in their careers while other, equally qualified people just run in place. "People skills" usually make the crucial difference. Use individuals you respect as role models or mentors. They will show you the obvious and not-so-obvious skills needed for successful careers. Adopt their traits as your own.

3. Never Allow Money to Determine What You Do and Become

Far too many of us become consumed by the desire to obtain money. We become slaves to it. We are willing to do anything to obtain it, regardless of whether it's right or wrong. We sacrifice our health, family and friends to obtain money. We abandon religious and moral beliefs for the opportunity to obtain it. We forfeit our values and who we are for the sake of money.

We destroy the most important aspect of ourselves when we allow our desire for money to turn us into someone we despise. Can you imagine living for 24 hours a day, day in, day out, year after year, with someone you despise? That's what happens when we allow our quest for money to turn us into someone we dislike. You are out of control when your desire to earn money does not allow you the time to relax and enjoy yourself and your family.

Too many people spend their lives creating fortunes, then die before they have a chance to enjoy it. They become so preoccupied with making money they neglect their personal well-being. They often betray their moral beliefs. The dollar becomes their religion and their god. They do not consider the consequences of their actions; they only consider the short-term benefits. These individuals have no problem stealing, swindling or taking advantage of others to make money. People who are solely guided by money are never willing to help others. They never volunteer their time unless they stand to profit by their actions.

There are many people out there with more money than they can spend in a hundred lifetimes and yet they are unhappy. You read about them in the papers every day — professional athletes, movie stars, singers, self-made millionaires, individuals who win lotteries, and so on. They have drug problems and emotional problems, commit suicide or murder, and get divorced. This shows that money itself does not solve life's problems.

When our actions are guided entirely by money, we live a selfish and disappointing life. There is nothing wrong with making money. We should all strive to be wealthy. We must understand, though, that success and happiness cannot be created by what we own or how much money we have. These qualities are determined by the type of person we become during the process of earning our living. Have we enriched the lives of others? Did we help others without concern for pay? You have to live with yourself 24 hours a day for the rest of your life. Become a person you can be proud to love.

4. Seek, Recognize, and Utilize Opportunities

The reason for the failure of most careers is an inability to recognize and use opportunities. Most individuals incorrectly believe that opportunities present themselves as opportunities. We waste time looking for signs that read "Opportunities Here."

Opportunities are rarely so obvious. In fact, many career opportunities present themselves as problems or obstacles that must be overcome. When we see these situations, we dread them. Most of us don't want to be bothered with problems. We would rather walk away from them. Here is a typical example that you may have encountered yourself:

A young woman went for an interview at a large, prestigious company. At the close of their meeting, the interviewer said he would call her with his decision in a week's time. Two weeks came and went — and no phone call. After several weeks and still no response from the company, the young woman got angry. Obviously, they had chosen another candidate for the position, which was disappointing. But she was also annoyed by the interviewer's poor manners. His failure to call when he said he would was unprofessional, and just plain rude.

Many people encountering this situation would have just stewed in silence and tried to get over their disappointment. But this young woman decided to do something about it. She called up the person who had interviewed her. It took a few tries to get through to him. When she did, she took a deep breath and calmly asked why he had failed to call her as promised. Unsatisfied with the response from the interviewer, she wrote a professional letter explaining why she felt she had been treated improperly and why it reflected negatively on the company. She addressed it to the president of the company. As a result of her assertive action, this young woman ended up being offered another position elsewhere in the company.

This story shows how unhappy situations can turn out to be opportunities if we respond to them actively rather than passively. We must not see problems as obstacles but challenges and opportunities to advance our careers and lives.

5. Learn to Take Worthwhile Risks

Success does not happen by chance or by luck. Success will never come if you wait for it. Some of us believe we will achieve success because we are good people or because we deserve it. This is not only foolish but dangerous. Waiting for a miracle or a change of luck is a major factor in the failure of careers. It prevents us from taking action when it is most needed.

Success never happens by accident or luck, or because we are deserving or did good deeds. Success happens when an individual takes reasonable risks. Risk takers don't wait for things to happen, they *make* things happen. When you create the conditions you want, you control your destiny and determine the success of your career.

It's unfortunate that most of us think of risks as something we should avoid. This could not be further from the truth. When we take risks, we distinguish ourselves from our peers. Remember, *you will not be noticed for doing the same things that everyone else does.*

It's important to distinguish worthwhile risks from foolish risks. Successful individuals do not take foolish risks, but realize there is a greater danger in not taking risks when the potential rewards outweigh potential losses. Instead of asking if they can afford to take the risk, they ask themselves if they can afford *not* to take the risk.

Risk takers are considered dynamic and visionary. They show personal power and a keen sense for making the right decisions. They don't wait for things to happen; they make them happen. They view options objectively from all points of view, putting aside their personal likes or dislikes. They determine which conditions will provide the best results. They know that what was the best approach yesterday may be inappropriate today. People with successful careers ask themselves four questions prior to taking risks:

1. What is the worst thing that could happen?
2. What is the best thing that could happen?
3. What probably *will* happen?
4. Can I afford not to take the risk?

By answering these four questions, you may realize that what at first appeared a great risk is actually not a risk at all. By using the answers to these questions you can examine your options. Your answers provide the wisdom and confidence to know which risks to take and which ones to avoid.

MAKING DIFFICULT DECISIONS

In this chapter we've seen that creating a successful career means taking control of our lives. It means making decisions and acting on them, rather than letting circumstances dictate our choices. This is rarely easy. No one has the answer to every problem or question. We will be faced with dilemmas where there are no right or wrong answers.

We must use our instincts and common sense to make appropriate decisions. We must make decisions based on our values, even when the outcome is not what we desire. When we make tough decisions based on reasons other than our values, we lose ourselves and the person we hope to become. Finding success in our careers at the sacrifice of our families and personal lives is a poor choice.

You have to live with the person you are for the rest of your life. Making the right decisions about your career may cost you money, aggravation and so-called friends in the short run. But in the end, the right decision brings long-term wealth, happiness, and true friends.

Chapter 2

Resumés
that Produce Results

*Do not attempt to do a thing unless you are sure of your-
self; but do not relinquish it simply because someone else is
not sure of you.*

—STEWART E. WHITE

As discussed in chapter 1, you need to establish your career goals
before you start looking for employment. Proceeding without
goals and a career plan is like traveling without a map — you'll
probably end up lost. Following the suggestions in chapter 1, devise
a plan and write it out. Once you have a satisfactory plan, you can
begin your career-building journey.

Before you apply for a position, be prepared. Being prepared starts
with a good resumé. How do we define a good resumé? A good
resumé must be a "best seller." A best-selling resumé quickly catch-
es the reader's attention, and sells you and your qualifications to
potential employers. It's your resumé that distinguishes you from
the crowd. A best-selling resumé generates interviews. A generic
resumé will get you nowhere in today's competitive employment
market.

See your resumé as a "work of art" that creates excitement in all
who gaze upon it. As in all works of art, pay close attention to col-
ors, space, lines, and details. Words must create pictures, excitement,
and interest. The format and design of your resumé must attract
readers. Use different fonts of various sizes, space and lines to catch
the reader's eye. Like all masterpieces, resumés require trial and
error before the perfect final product is achieved.

Resumés must be designed to create the interest that generates interviews. If your resumé fails to create interest, you will not have the opportunity to show your skills and abilities, regardless of how qualified or talented you are. Applicants often fail to invest sufficient time in creating the best possible resumé, yet it is among the most powerful tools available for obtaining the position you desire. Often it is the only opportunity you have to sell yourself to employers. After you finish reading this chapter you will know how to write and design a best-selling resumé.

Choose a Format that Fits

Before creating your resumé, choose a resumé format that best fits your background — education, experience, employment stability, expertise, etc. There are five acceptable resumé formats:

Chronological resumés are best if you have an excellent work history with no significant employment gaps. They work well when your work history shows professional growth and stability. Chronological resumés also work well when you are seeking positions in your area of experience. Chronological resumés emphasize work history. They list the names of employers and positions, starting with your present or most recent position. If you've worked for a company with a prestigious name, it adds credibility to your resumé.

Functional resumés are the best choice if you want to emphasize capabilities and highlight major accomplishments and skills. They allow you to de-emphasize employment gaps, employment hopping, poor work experience, or little or no education. Functional resumés are also suitable for candidates who are making career changes and lack actual work experience. Functional resumés allow you to emphasize volunteer work in the area you desire employment in. You can effectively use this to compensate for the lack of work experience in a field.

Targeted resumés are for employment in a specialized line of work. They are written in specific terms and focused on a particular position. They narrow employment opportunities. Use different targeted resumés for each employment field you wish to enter. This is necessary if you are applying to different fields because of diverse interests and talents.

Combination resumés take the best features of the chronological and functional resumés and combines them in a single format. This format allows you to present the best components of your work history, capabilities, and accomplishments. It allows you to de-emphasize negative components in these areas.

Alternative resumés are only used for specific situations, such as when you've been unemployed for long periods — for example, if you were a housewife or househusband for 20 years and have little or no formal work experience. Alternative resumés can also be used in fields that require creativity and imagination, such as advertising or marketing. You can also use this format if you can identify position requirements and match them to your skills or experience.

Familiarize yourself with each resumé format. Deciding which resumé format best fits your background and needs is critical. Your experience, education, and expertise will determine this.

Get Reviewers to Select Your Resumé

Notice I've used the word "create" instead of "write" your resumé. After reading this chapter you will learn words alone are not sufficient to make a resumé a best seller. Looks are important when it comes to your resumé. Its appearance, not its content, is what first attracts readers. This is critical because, on average, 55 individuals apply for each advertised position. Let's face it, no one wants to read 55 or more boring resumés.

Know what interviewers look for in resumés. A stylish and bold resumé design for a graphic designer is inappropriate for a conservative stock broker or accounting firm. The actual design of your resumé is determined by:

- The personality of the industry
- Your level of experience and age
- The type of position you are seeking

Each industry's personality determines whether your resumé should be bold, stylish, formal, or unconventional in its design. Its appearance will either attract readers or turn them away. Therefore, know and understand your intended audience's taste. What some consider a work of art will be considered trash by others.

As you will see when I describe the resumé review process below, the recipient has little time to read a resumé. The more time it takes to read and comprehend a resumé, the more likely it will be discarded. Don't let your resumé's style or design get in the way of readability.

Your resumé must tell readers what type of person you are, what you do, and what you've accomplished. It must reflect your personality, skills, experience, and what you have to offer. Consider your resumé a painting of yourself. Is it vivid, do lines flow properly? Is it colorful and interesting? Does it draw you toward it or make you want to throw it away? Would you want to have this painting around you, day after day? Is this painting missing something or does something need to be removed? Is it too cluttered or does it have too much blank space?

Ask yourself this question: Does this painting (resumé) complement this wall (company) or does it belong somewhere else? Find out what type of employees prospective companies hire. Are they looking for aggressive individuals? If so, show you are aggressive on your resumé. Match your style of resumé to the style of the company. Have more than one style of resumé to fit the characteristics of different employers.

Here's what happens when an employer receives a large number of resumés for an opening:

Each resumé is given a quick review. Based on this review, the resumés are divided into three stacks. The first stack of resumés are strong candidates. The second stack is for not-so-strong candidates. The third stack is for the trash bin.

The resumés in the first stack are then read in detail. From this stack, resumés are selected for interviews. If a position pays $100,000 or less, usually five candidates are selected for interviews. If the position pays more than $100,000, usually ten to twelve candidates are selected for interviews. If the requisite number of resumés are selected from the first stack, the second stack may go unread. If the initial interviews do not work out, or fewer resumés than needed were selected from the first stack, the second stack of resumés is reviewed. If the remaining qualified candidates are found in the second stack, they are called for interviews.

Even when individuals are not interviewed or hired from the first and second stack of resumés, they are often saved for future consideration for positions within that department. Good resumés may be circulated throughout the company to fill other vacant positions. They are also used as back-up resumés if the candidate that is hired does not pass probation. One out of four new employees does not complete the probationary period.

This process shows that about 95 percent of resumés are initially rejected. How can we increase our chances of being among the 5 percent selected for interviews? Here are the four reasons resumés are selected for further review and interviews:

1. The appearance of the resumé
2. Ease of reading
3. Applicants show they are qualified for the position
4. The applicant is currently employed

1. Your Resumé's Appearance

To be successful, you must attract the reader to your resumé. Your resumé's appearance must be pleasing to the eye, brief, easy to read, and to the point. It must immediately show you are qualified for the position. Your resumé must show these qualities at a glance. Use a computer to produce your resumé. It will allow you to use different fonts and other design elements that will draw the reviewer's eye. If you are not proficient with a computer or don't have a good design sense, it may be a worthy investment to have a professional desktop publisher create a resumé for you.

Print your master resumé copies on a laser printer. Keep several master copies of your resumé. You will need more than one copy in case you lose or damage the master resumé you use to make copies. It is faster and more economical to have large quantities of copies made of your resumé than to laser print them. If you make copies of your resumé, make sure your master copy is perfect. If it has smudges or markings, discard it and use another one. Do not reduce the effectiveness of your resumé by using a copier that makes poor copies. Resumés that are badly copied and poorly prepared suggest a lack of self respect and pride in your work. This is not the message you want to send to potential employers.

2. Ease of Reading

Resumés must never look cluttered. The proper use of blank space is critical to resumés. Proper spacing makes resumés easier to read. Remember, less is best when you write your resumé. Get directly to the point. Don't waste words. Choose your words carefully.

One-page resumés are best. It may not be possible to keep to one page if you have numerous employers and they all relate to your current search. Only then should your resumé be one and a half pages long. If you have numerous awards, accomplishments and other important career highlights, list them on separate pages as an addendum to your resumé. Resumés should never be more than a page and a half long. If your resumé is longer, rewrite it. Only include information of interest to the employer you are applying to.

Collect good resumés and incorporate their ideas into yours. Have qualified individuals critique your resumé to determine if it is too wordy or too brief, interesting or boring.

3. Show You Are Qualified for the Position

The number one rule for interviewers is to never interview candidates who are not qualified. If a company is advertising for a Controller and your resumé shows you are an Accounts Payable Clerk, they will not interview you. This does not mean that if you don't have all the qualifications you will not be hired. It does mean you must have the most important qualifications. Your resumé must also show you can perform the work.

Employers generally cannot find candidates with all the qualifications they desire. In these situations they hire candidates who most closely match what they are looking for. Match your resumé as closely as possible to the skills and experience required for the position you seek. If you are making a career change emphasize similar skills and experience. Your resumé must show that your existing skills and experience can be used in the position you seek.

Match Your Resumé to the Position

Creating the most impressive resumé in the world is a waste of time if it is not compatible with the position you seek. It will not generate interviews. This is why it is important to have more than one resumé on hand.

Having different versions of a resumé is particularly helpful for individuals who have diverse backgrounds. Let's say you have experience in selling, management and accounting. You should have a multi-purpose resumé showing you have experience in all three of these areas. When you apply for a position that requires all three of these skills, it is ideal.

On the other hand, many positions require specialized skills. If you are applying for a sales position, your sales experience would be your selling point. Your management and accounting skills or experience would be of little interest to this employer. In fact, this may work against you. In situations such as this, it would be better to have another resumé that emphasizes your sales skills and experience. The same would be true if you have an extensive background in accounting finance (accounts payable and receivable, general ledger, payroll, taxes and financial statement preparation). When applying for a general accounting position, your resumé should emphasize your general accounting skills and experience.

Having several resumé versions makes you more marketable. Different versions allow you to highlight those skills and experiences most important for that job. A single, all-purpose resumé can't do this.

When you have more than one version of your resumé, keep track of where you send them. You never want to go to an interview and give someone the wrong version of your resumé. It will make you look bad, and you will not be hired.

Make sure each version of your resumé is factual. Most people add some fluff to their resumé. If you slightly exaggerate your skills and experience but are fully capable of performing the work, this results in no harm. Always put your skills, experience, and accomplishments in the best light; don't be overly modest.

On the other hand you should never list skills on your resumé that you do not have and are unwilling to put forth the effort to learn. If you do, you're just setting yourself up for disaster and professional suicide. It is a frustrating experience to be placed in a position that is beyond your capabilities. To be terminated for incompetence is also an unpleasant experience.

It's also a bad idea to fib about work experience or educational qualifications. After a number of publicized cases of employees with faked qualifications, employers are being more careful about checking them. You could find yourself in court one day if you misrepresent yourself in this way.

Mild exaggeration isn't always to your benefit either. In general, employers prefer not to hire applicants who are over qualified for a position. They believe over-qualified employees will continue to look for employment after they hire them. They believe they will leave when they find positions more compatible with their education, training, and skills.

You may want to think twice about applying for a position that's not going to make full use of your abilities. However, if you are over qualified for a position that you're sure you want to apply for, do not show all degrees or experience. Match your resumé and application with the skills, education and experience required for the particular position you're applying for. If you leave any information out of your resumé for fear of appearing over qualified, remember to leave it out at your interview as well.

The exception to this general rule is the public-sector employer. City, state, and federal governments look for bargains. They are non-profit organizations. They *like* to hire people who are over qualified. The more you have, the more they like it. When applying for a government position, show everything you've got. They will gladly hire over-qualified individuals.

4. Always Show You Are Employed

A resumé indicating that you are unemployed immediately places you at a disadvantage. It automatically raises red flags and negative questions in the interviewer's mind: Why are you unemployed? Were you fired? Why were you fired? Did you have problems with your former employer and employees? If you were not fired, why did you leave? Were you asked to leave? Why did you leave your present employment without first having another position?

Such questions and the subsequent doubts they raise are often the reason you are not selected for interviews. If two equally qualified candidates apply for a position, one employed and the other not, the employed candidate is looked upon more favorably. Our society places a stigma on the unemployed. We believe something is wrong with them or they did something wrong. We think they are shiftless, lazy troublemakers who are up to no good. These suspicions and doubts make employers hesitant about hiring the unemployed. A one-second hesitation is all that is needed to place you in the 95 percent rejection file. Due to fierce competition and legal labor costs (unemployment cost, worker compensation, and law suits), employers are cautious when they hire employees.

Like it or not, there is a bias against the unemployed. People trust the judgment of others. They want employees other people want. The unemployed appear to be a greater risk, regardless if it's true or not. You will not get the benefit of the doubt because they do not know you.

It is not impossible to be hired if you are unemployed, but it reduces your chances. Even if you are hired, it reduces your chances of obtaining the best salary and compensation package. When you are employed, it gives you greater bargaining power and allows you the opportunity to negotiate the best deal possible.

The way to overcome this problem is to never apply for a position without showing you are employed. "But, the reason I'm applying is because I'm unemployed!" you may be yelling in exasperation at this point. Calm down and read the following suggestions.

Sign Up with a Temporary Employment Agency

As I've stated above, you improve your opportunities of being hired if you are employed. However, "employment" doesn't have to mean regular, permanent employment. When you become unemployed, sign up with a temporary employment agency while you're searching for a permanent position. Registering with more than one agency is a good idea — it increases your opportunities to work.

Even if you get dull assignments, doing temporary work can bring in much-needed cash. Having a place to go to each day can also be beneficial psychologically. And if you work for temporary employment agencies, you are their employee. You can use their name on your resumé as your employer. List the dates you signed up as your employment dates. Assignments are usually of short duration. Once assignments are completed the agency finds employees other temporary assignments. You do not have to show gaps between assignments.

Never take temporary work lightly. Avoid the mistake of believing you don't have to do your best because it is temporary. Temporary workers are often hired permanently if they impress their clients. Even if a client cannot offer you a permanent position, they may be able to provide you with valuable references and networking sources that can help you obtain the position you really want.

Start a Business

Starting a business is another way of filling in periods of unemployment. It need not take a large investment — you can use your home as your office. Computers allow many small, home-based businesses to successfully compete with large companies. A few examples are:

- Medical billing services
- Import/export business
- Consulting services

- Web page design
- Mail order
- Accounting & taxes

The possibilities of working at home are endless with new technological advancements. You do not have to indicate it's a home-based business on your resumé. However, you do have to show that is a legitimate business.

There are other benefits to starting a home-based business when you are out of work (and even when you're not). You can write off portions of former personal expenses (consult a tax accountant to learn how to do this). Home businesses are sources of income and teach owners new skills. They provide experience that can be helpful in future employment. If you are successful, you may decide to continue your business after you find employment. You may become so successful that you decide to quit working for others.

There are numerous books, magazines, courses and organizations that can help you start your own business. See the Resources section of this book for some suggestions.

Do Volunteer Work

Being employed doesn't have to mean you get paid for what you do. Any community has an endless need for all types of volunteer help. Check your local government's volunteer bureau. You may be surprised at the range of positions available. As well as making you feel good, this employment can be listed on your resumé. You don't have to say it is a voluntary position, but doing so may look good, especially to employers who pride themselves on community involvement.

Volunteer work can also provide you with references and networking opportunities. Some organizations also have paid employees; you may end up being hired by the people you do volunteer work for.

Household Engineers

Household engineers are the mothers or fathers who have stayed home to raise children and run their households. If you have been a household engineer, you may have little or no outside work experience. On paper it may look as if you've been "unemployed." This does not mean you have no skills of value to employers, however.

Regrettably, society tends to look down on the work stay-at-home moms and dads do. Because you are not paid, your work is undervalued. Some people don't see it as "work" at all. This is obviously unfair, but unfortunately, many employers share these opinions. Therefore, do not state on your resumé that you are a housewife or househusband. It may lead employers to overlook important skills and abilities you have to offer. Instead, show the skills you've acquired from your work at home. If you are applying for a position with children, emphasize your child care skills. If you handle home finances — bookkeeping, budgeting, accounts payable (personal bills) — highlight your accounting skills.

Show how you can apply your household skills to the position you are applying for. If you've performed volunteer work and gained valuable experience through it, reflect it in your resumés. The organizational ability and stamina it takes to run a home efficiently are qualities every employer values. Don't sell yourself short.

Create an Interest in Yourself

In addition to containing the essential criteria listed above, your resumé must sell you to a potential employer. You want to show not only that you are eminently qualified for a particular position, but that you will be an asset to the company as a whole. Your resumé must not only state what you've done but emphasize major accomplishments during your employment. Ideal resumés should show how your employment had a positive impact on your previous employers (increased sales and profits, reduced expenses, etc.).

Make your resumé exciting. Use action words and phrases, such as "accomplished," "succeeded," "achieved," "implemented," "successfully turned around," and so on. Include promotions, awards and honors that you received from former employers, schools and volunteer organizations.

Make use of important titles. Remember to use titles interviewers recognize. If your present position has a nebulous title, get it changed. Do this as soon as possible, even if you are not looking for employment. You never know when you'll have to find another position. If your employer is in dire straits and cannot give you a raise, ask for a change in title instead. Often they'll allow you to choose your own title. Be sure to pick one that reflects responsibility and accomplishment. Your title will be important when looking for future employment.

Former fancy, unrecognizable titles mean little or nothing to new employers. The title "Senior Executive Coordinator," for example, may sound impressive at a former company, but would make most resumé readers wonder what you are talking about.

Remember, you want your resumé to create interest at a glance. Show titles in capital and bold letters so they stand out. Do the same for prestigious companies you've worked for, as well as degrees and schools when appropriate.

Applicants often show objectives on their resumés. If you state your objective, make sure it fits with the company's objectives. If your objective suggests you want to progress quickly and the company needs someone to stay in a position for several years, this one statement could eliminate you.

Find out as much as you can about a company before you send them your resumé. Talk to current and former employees of the company you are applying to. Find out what type of people the company hires. This is easy to do if you know someone who works for the company. If you don't, visit the company or one of its offices. Observe what type of people work there, how they act, speak and dress. When possible, speak with employees who work there. Another possibility is to research newspaper and magazine articles for vital information about the company. If you don't know how to go about this, ask a librarian. The Internet can also provide vital information, such as press releases, articles and announcements. All this information will help you produce the best resumé for approaching that employer.

Never be satisfied with an old resumé, and don't just update the current section. Review your entire resumé objectively. What do you like or dislike about it? Never read your resumé just from your viewpoint. Read your resumé from a prospective employer's view. Ask yourself, Would I hire this person sight unseen?

If you are not getting results from your resumé, redo it. Keep a log of which resumés result in interviews. Use the resumés that work. Have several versions of your resumé. Make sure your resumé is the best it can possibly be. Always look for ways to improve it. Be willing to experiment until you have a resumé that works for you. Your resumé is only working if it generates interviews.

If you have written an ineffective resumé and lack the ability to create a better one, make an investment in yourself and pay someone to create one or more for you. Make sure you are comfortable with the resumé they produce. If you are unwilling to pay someone to create a resumé, consider this: The money you saved by not using a professional may cost you the position you desired.

Filling Out an Application

Some employers require applicants to complete application forms prior to interviewing them. Before going to an interview get a standard job application form and fill it in. Bring the completed form with you to the interview. You can use it as a guide when filling in the employer's form. It will help ensure that your application form is complete, error-free and neatly filled in.

When employers review the application forms the first things they look for are legibility, neatness and completeness. Reviewers do not waste time trying to decipher bad handwriting or searching for incomplete information. This shows the applicant does sloppy work and does not follow instructions. A neatly completed application suggests a good work attitude. It also shows you follow directions.

Never leave blank spaces on your application. If a question does not apply to you write "non-applicable" (N/A) in the space. Never answer questions on applications by writing "See attached resumé." Do attach a copy of your resumé to the application, though.

Application reviewers will likely check the reasons you give for having left your previous position. Never use these three reasons for leaving your employer:

- **They did not like me**
- **I quit**
- **I was fired**

When reviewers read these responses, they think the candidate did something wrong. Also take care in using phrases such as "I was laid off, "or "I was let go due to restructuring or downsizing." Interviewers know many candidates use these excuses when they've been fired. If you use these terms, use them wisely. Here are some better answers for why you left your employer:

- **Position was not challenging**

- General layoff
- To render greater service
- Seeking opportunity

Always Be Ready for a New Employer

Every year, rewrite your resumé, even if you are not seeking employment. Update it so that you will be prepared for opportunities. The best opportunities often occur when you least expect them.

Another reason to update your resumé is to determine whether your present skills are marketable. Have a look at the help wanted ads to see what kinds of skills employers in your field are currently seeking. Compare them with those on your resumé — if you had to start hunting for a new position tomorrow, would your skills be in demand? The best time to upgrade your skills is before you need to find new employment. If you are unable to produce a resumé that shows you have marketable skills and experience, you need to take steps to correct this situation.

Identify the skills you need to be competitive in your field. Create a plan to stay current with new developments. Take steps to acquire the necessary skills and training. Indicate on your resumé that you are enrolled in classes to acquire these skills. As soon as you have completed a course, be sure to include it on your updated resumé.

Always keep on top of changes in your chosen field. Read related magazines and journals; join professional associations and attend their meetings; take workshops and seminars. By staying informed you will be able to anticipate any major changes in the skills required for your field and prepare yourself accordingly. It is in your best interest not to play catch-up in learning these skills. Employers want employees who are trained, not employees who *plan* to be trained. If you lack skills, you limit yourself to entry-level positions or a place in the rejection file.

Get Computerized

Do your resumé on a computer. This allows you to make changes quickly and easily. If you don't own a computer, now is the time to purchase one. Computers improve in speed and other capabilities every year, so it is difficult to give definite advice as to what you should look for. Consult a computer-literate friend and magazines like *Consumer Reports* to determine what you need. In any case you will need a modem to access the Internet and to circulate your resumé. Make it easier to communicate with prospective employers by having an E-mail address and fax number. Include these on your resumé.

Make a smart investment in yourself: If you currently do not have computer skills, start acquiring them today. You cannot compete with others if you lack these skills. It's been said it is not who learns computer programs best but who learns them first that will be the most successful.

At minimum, learn to use a word processing program, a spreadsheet program, a data base program and the Internet (i.e., E-mail, browsers such as Netscape, search engines such as Yahoo). Software programs have become extremely powerful and easy to learn. There are usually two or three popular programs of each of these types of software; you don't need to learn all of them, just learn one really well. They tend to have the same basic features, so it doesn't take long to adapt to a different one if need be.

Having a computer at home will make it much easier to learn and practice these programs. Save your money and buy the best one you can afford. If you simply can't afford your own computer, take classes where computers are provided. Learn on a friend's computer. There are places where you can rent computers and laser printers by the hour if you are unable to access them by other means. Check the Yellow Pages.

Electronic Applicant Tracking

Technology is not only changing the way we work but also the way employers select applicants for openings. Computers are now searching for and selecting resumés to be considered for interviews. This technology is called "electronic applicant tracking." It is currently being used by major companies and is expected to grow in popularity. Resumés are scanned into employers' computer systems. Artificial intelligence then "reads" the resumé and extracts pertinent elements such as

- Name, Address, Phone Number
- Work History
- Experience
- Skills
- Accomplishments
- Education
- Objectives
- Previous employers

Once your resumé is scanned, it may be kept in the company's active files for years. Their computer will even review it for positions you did not apply for. This makes it easier to be considered for positions and provides more opportunities to be hired. It is critical that you create a resumé that will maximize the computer's ability to scan it. Some features that make resumés difficult to scan include small or unusual fonts, columns or unusual page layouts, light type, printing on dark paper, and graphics and lines. Here are ways to produce a "scannable" resumé:

- Use a laser printer to print your resumé.
- Use standard fonts (Times, Helvetica, Courier).
- Use white or light-colored paper.
- Submit only high-quality copies.

- Use bold type for headings.
- Use single lines for name, address, phone.
- Make sure letters do not touch.
- Avoid underlines, italics, reverse text and shadows.
- Place your name at the top of the page.
- Don't condense letter or line spacing.
- Do not fold or staple your resumé.
- Use font sizes between 10 and 14 points.

Resumés must also be written to get "hits." A hit occurs when one or more of your skills matches the computer's search criteria for a particular position. Do the following to increase the number of hits your resumé will score:

- Include key words that define skills, experience, positions, education, accomplishments.
- Avoid vague words; use descriptive words and acceptable industry jargon and acronyms.
- Use words that show you are qualified for the position.
- If you know the resumé is to be scanned be more descriptive and expand it to two pages.
- Load up with words required for a position (Microsoft Word, Access, Excel, WordPerfect, HTML).
- Use common headings (i.e., Objectives, Degrees, Skills, Strengths, Honors, Education, Licenses, etc.).

Following the search criteria for a position, computers select a predetermined number of resumés. These will be reviewed by a human being who determines which applicants will be selected for interviews.

Now that you know resumés are not just selected by human beings but by computers as well, be prepared for both situations. When you research companies find out if they scan or do computer searches to select applicants from job banks. If you can determine which method is used, select the appropriate type of resumé to submit. You can play it safe and send one eye-appealing resumé (for humans) and one designed to be scanned (for computers). Today most resumés are still selected the old-fashioned way, but in years to come this may change. In any case, you will still need a visually appealing resumé for actual interviews.

* * *

I'll end this chapter by reminding you of the important features of a resumé. If your resumé quickly and easily shows these features, you will be selected for interviews.

- It must be attractive and appealing to the eye.
- Readers must see your skills, selling points and experience within eight seconds or less.
- It must be brief, easy to read, and interesting.
- It must show you are a perfect fit for the position offered.
- Many of the rules that apply to paper resumés (manually selected) do not apply to resumés used in electronic applicant tracking. Know the difference and when the appropriate format should be used.

Once your resumé fulfills these requirements, congratulations — you have written a best-selling resumé! Writing a best-selling resumé is a process that takes time. It may require learning new skills and making changes. This is called personal and professional growth. Taking the time to create a best-selling resumé will result in obtaining the interviews and positions you want.

Chapter 3

Generating Interviews

Labor is man's greatest function. He is nothing, he can do nothing, he can achieve nothing, he can fulfill nothing, without working.

—ORVILLE DEWEY

IN CHAPTER 2 we gave a lot of consideration to how to best present ourselves to employers through our resumés. Before we submit our first resumé or make our first contact, we must ask ourselves some important questions. Answering these questions prevents the waste of valuable time and energy. It will weed out positions and companies that are not suitable for us.

We sometimes worry too much about whether we will be suitable for an employer, and not enough about whether an employer is suitable for *us*. There must be compatibility between our needs and those of our employers. Only by selecting employers who meet our criteria will we find success and happiness in our careers. Here are some questions you should ask yourself as you consider which employers to approach:

- How far am I willing to commute?
- Am I willing to relocate (within or outside of state)?
- What is the minimum salary I would accept?
- If I pursue this position would it have a negative or positive effect on my future (education, family, health, happiness, etc.)?

- Would I enjoy working for this company?
- Will this employer provide what I am looking for?

These questions are not all-inclusive. Based on our likes, skills and expectations we may need to ask additional questions. Answer these questions carefully and truthfully — remember, this process is for your benefit. Write your answers down. They will help you keep your perspective should you receive an offer from an unsuitable employer.

If you've been unemployed or underemployed, or are desperate to change employers, it may be very tempting to accept the first position you are offered. Doing so may be a relief in the short run, but could damage your career prospects over time. If you end up in a situation where you are unhappy, or a long commute is wearing you down, or your family life suffers due to your long working hours, you'll quickly get stressed out. You won't be working to your optimum level. You won't be making the good impression needed to land promotions and raises. You may even end up holding a pink slip. It is important to resist the temptation to take any job you can find. Having your written career plan on hand, along with the criteria outlined in the questions above, will help you keep on track.

BEST INTERVIEW SOURCES

You have your career plan. You have a stock of carefully produced resumés. You have a list of criteria for the type of employer you are looking for and the geographical area in which you want to work. Now you need to get your foot in the door. Having an impeccable resumé is one thing; getting it in front of the right person is quite another. How do you get someone to call you up for an interview?

The one thing you don't do is wait for others to tell you where to send your resumés. Waiting at home for the phone to ring does not generate interviews or build careers. We are powerless when we wait for opportunities. Work to create opportunities for yourself. Don't just rely on conventional methods to land interviews. Never allow fear or embarrassment to prevent you from using unorthodox methods to find employment. They are often the most successful and provide an edge by showing you are different from the crowd. Keep in mind, however, that the techniques you use must be tasteful, ethical, and legal.

You may be unaware of the many employment sources available. The conventional job-hunting route is to look for advertised positions. While this method may result in interviews, it is not always the most effective way to make contact with potential employers. A study of hiring practices was done by Harvard University sociologist Mark S. Granovetter (*Getting a Job: A Study of Contacts and Careers.* Cambridge: University Press, 1974). Granovetter's study focused primarily on how professional, managerial and technical individuals find employment. The results were as follows:

Networking	74.5%
Advertising	10.0%
Search firms/ Employment agencies	9.0%

More recent studies have confirmed these results. Let's look at these three sources for generating interviews — networking, newspaper and magazine advertising, and employment agencies.

Networking

Networking is by far the most effective method for obtaining positions and building a career. Networking helps to penetrate the "hidden" job market.

What is networking? Networking is an informal system whereby individuals having common interests assist each other in the exchange of information and developing contacts, or as sources for employment. It is using personal contacts to help you reach a goal. Imagine yourself at the center of a web. You have immediate connections to a certain number of people — family, friends, co-workers, business associates, and so on. Each of those people in turn has his or her own contacts who may or may not be known to you. Networking is an active process of reaching these unknown people through your immediate circle of contacts. Your friend may not be hiring at his company, but maybe he one of his suppliers has an opening that might be suitable for you.

Many job opportunities like these are unknown to the public because they are never publicly advertised. This is why relying on newspaper help wanted listings is not very effective. Networking is usually the only way outsiders learn of these jobs.

Employers are always looking for replacements before they need them. They usually don't like to have a position open for long. However, advertising is sometimes awkward or inefficient. If they're planning to fire people, they don't want to let them know in advance by placing ads for their positions. They may have a high achiever they wish to promote quickly to a position where better use can be made of his or her abilities. Opportunities or competitive threats can arise quickly, requiring speedy hirings. For these reasons, employers sometimes prefer to hire from within their organizations or through personal recommendations. Networking is the only way to find out about these openings.

Regardless of how effective networking is, it will not get results if it is not done properly. To get the most from networking never network for the sole purpose of obtaining a position. Networking is not a one-way relationship where people help you and you give nothing in return. You must help others during the process of networking.

Never request payment for helping or assisting others when networking. If you request or expect payment it becomes a business relationship, not a networking one. People may need you today but you may need them more tomorrow. We accrue points and build relationships when we help others. Most individuals will gladly return your favors.

Reliable networking relationships take time to build. The best time to build strong and lasting networks is before you need them. It gives you the opportunity to develop trust and familiarity. Once this is achieved, people are more inclined to go out of their way to help you, your friends and your family members.

Networks are an important means of exchanging ideas and learning the latest information about your field. They help you keep current with new trends, developments, and techniques. They will help you find answers to problems and allow you to meet experts in your field. They also provide opportunities for establishing reputations in your industry.

Developing interests and networks outside your employer is essential. Do this while you are employed. Employees who devote themselves entirely to work have difficulty finding employment when they are unemployed because they have limited resources. They never bothered to develop networks to help them. Never allow yourself to be in position of being unemployed and not having a network in place to help you. This reduces your chances of finding new employment by 75 percent. Let's look at some ways you can get started on your networking.

Business Contacts and Associates

Business contacts and associates can provide valuable employment leads. Develop business and social relationships with them. To be of assistance, they must be aware of your abilities and skills through a prior relationship with you or by your reputation. Often they will inform you of career opportunities when they hear of positions that match your skills. If you ask for assistance, they will gladly give it.

Always perform at your best whenever you work with others, even if it's for a single occasion. We often have only one chance to impress others. We never know when we will need others for leads or references. One employer described an interesting recruitment technique that shows why you should always be on your toes: Whenever an employee of another company provides her with good service, she hands them her business card and tells them to give her a call if they are ever looking for work.

However, simply doing your best work is not always enough to draw attention to yourself as a potential candidate for employment. There are several ways to approach business associates or contacts. Try sending out subtle feelers to gauge their response. During conversation, show you want to make a career change or are seeking new employment. You may receive an employment offer or a valuable lead.

Another approach is to be more direct in asking for assistance in finding a position. Ask the people you meet to inform you of positions available where they work. Ask if they would circulate your resumé, particularly among their Personnel Department and any department heads who need employees with your skills. Make sure they are aware of the type of position or career you want. Let them know what your expectations are and the type of companies you are interested in. The more they know about your skills and expectations, the better they can help you. They won't be wasting your time and theirs on positions that are not suitable. Ask for advice on enhancing your chances for success. Many of these individuals can give you valuable information and suggestions.

Always be professional when approaching business contacts and associates for their assistance. Make sure you approach them at an appropriate time. Never try to pressure individuals to help you. If you do, they will avoid you in the future. Conduct yourself so that others feel comfortable providing you with a reference. Never do anything to make them look bad. Always show appreciation for the help of others.

Social Events

Social events are valuable settings for developing contacts and leads when used properly. It is important that we do not make nuisances of ourselves. We all dread individuals who want to do nothing but talk shop, conduct business, or ask for favors when we are trying to enjoy ourselves. We avoid these people like the plague. Be careful not to create this impression when you are developing leads.

We can avoid this situation by following some simple rules. Remember social events are *social* events. Never try to make them business meetings. When you speak with others keep your conversation on a social level. Find out as much as you can about the people you meet. Ask questions about them and their work. Keep your conversation as friendly as possible. Create rapport during conversation. Listen carefully.

Determine if the people you meet can provide possible leads or career opportunities. During or at the end of your conversation, inform them you would be interested in speaking with them about their work at a more appropriate time. They may volunteer to provide you with assistance. If they do not, ask if it would be possible to call or visit them later. Stress that you would like to find out more information about their field of work. Do not suggest you are looking for employment at this time unless they volunteer to assist you. Ask for business cards or phone numbers to contact them. Make sure you have business cards to give out.

It is important that these contacts remember your name. Always make your acquaintance memorable and enjoyable. Set up a specific date and time when you can call or meet to follow up on your conversation. Write the information down. Before you call or meet them, come up with three or four brief questions that will yield the information you need. If you've scheduled a meeting, call a day or two in advance to confirm your appointment. If it must be changed, make sure you schedule a new date before you finish your conversation. If you do not reschedule it right then, you lose your momentum and may never have the opportunity again.

Always call or meet at the specified time and date. Be punctual. This displays professionalism and reliability. If a secretary screens your call, say that your call is expected. Introduce yourself and remind them where you met. At the start of the conversation thank them for taking the time to speak or meet with you.

Know what you want. Be brief, polite and appreciative and ask your four questions. After your questions are answered, determine the best way to use this information during your conversation or meeting. Now is the appropriate time to tell them about your skills and goals. If you are in a face-to-face meeting, give them a copy of your resumé. Ask if they can assist you. Determine if they have positions suitable for you. If the answer is yes, immediately set up an interview if it cannot be done then.

If positions are not available ask if they can refer you to other individuals who need your services. Try to obtain leads (companies, names, and phone numbers). Provide copies of your resumé to keep on file and to circulate within and outside their company. If you are speaking by phone, tell them you will send them copies. Be brief, courteous, and professional. This is critical, regardless of whether they help you or not. They may contact you with future positions or leads. Ask them to keep you under consideration for future openings that become available. Thank them again for their time, consideration, and help.

People appreciate politeness. It sets you apart from the crowd. Your good manners will be remembered — it will increase your chances for future employment. A day or two after your meeting, send a thank-you card. Thank-you cards are better than thank-you letters. People enjoy receiving cards. Thank-you cards take little time to read and are more personal. We are inclined to read a card before we read a letter. Include business cards and your home phone number to make it easy for them to contact you when positions or leads become available.

Do not become discouraged if you do not obtain immediate leads. This process develops valuable life-long contacts and will create future opportunities.

Organizations and Churches

Organizations, both secular and religious, can be excellent sources of employment leads. They provide opportunities to meet powerful, influential people who can hire you. Individuals who cannot hire you may be able to refer you to people who can.

Organizations such as community service clubs are established to help improve the lives of members and other individuals. Organizations are not just for making contacts. They give us the opportunity to see how successful people conduct themselves. They provide free information. Many organizations provide training for your career. Many encourage members to be mentors and sponsors to others. Some organizations have career placement facilities to help members find employment.

Some organizations have been established for a particular interest, others have broader goals. They allow you to meet people of diverse backgrounds. They expose members to a wide range of careers and opportunities. Members share common interests or bonds. There are many different organizations to help you.

Churches and temples are important organizations, not only for finding spiritual salvation but also for obtaining employment. You will meet individuals who will help you find the career you want. Many churches actively help members find employment. They are great sources for networking.

Attend meetings, join and use organizations and churches that will help you in your search. Speak with family, friends, and associates who can refer you to helpful organizations. If the organizations, clubs and religious group you belong to do not offer a career assistance service, show your initiative by setting one up.

Professional Associations

Every occupation has its attendant associations designed to benefit and promote its members and the profession. These associations develop standards and codes of ethics. They establish recruiting and training programs for new and existing professionals in their field.

Become actively involved in professional associations. They are excellent sources of employment leads and provide valuable insight into their fields. Important and helpful people are involved in professional associations. They provide mentors and sponsors to help you. You can find listings of thousands of professional associations in the *Directory of Associations* in the reference section of your local library.

Newspapers and Magazines

The classified employment section of your newspaper is the most common form of advertisement used to find employment and careers. It can be an excellent source of information and leads. Just be sure you make it work for you and not against you. It works against you if you apply for positions merely because they were advertised. Your search should be well planned and organized. Know in advance what field(s) you are interested in. Conduct your search in that direction. If you search the paper haphazardly and apply for anything that's available, you are looking for a job and not a career.

Use these tips to make your search more productive. Get to know on which days the best positions are advertised. It is generally Thursdays and Sundays. Many major papers issue a late Saturday paper that lists the Sunday classified employment section. If your city has a small local newspaper, don't make the mistake of limiting yourself to it. Use larger newspapers. They have the largest listing of classified employment opportunities. They list positions for a wider area than small newspapers. Many companies use larger newspapers because they obtain better results due to their larger circulation.

There are advantages and drawbacks to small local newspapers. They advertise fewer positions and are used by smaller companies, but fewer applicants apply for them. The advertised positions are generally local and closer to home. Larger newspapers list a larger selection of positions, and large, prestigious companies usually prefer to advertise in them, but competition is greater because more people apply.

If you are willing to relocate to another city or state, obtain copies of the newspapers in those areas. If you have friends or families in those areas have them fax or over-night mail the classified sections to you as soon as possible. Another excellent source is your local library. Most libraries subscribe to many local, regional and national daily newspapers. If your local library branch does not, visit your city's main library. Use a variety of newspapers. Find out the days on which the largest ads are published. Review them carefully. Look for positions that pertain to your career.

Maintain a list of the employers to whom you've sent resumés. Keep track of company names, addresses, contact names, phone numbers, and dates (date sent, date called, etc.). Develop a follow-up file. When you send out a resumé, record a follow-up date on your calendar. If you do not receive a response by that date, call the company and find out if the position is still available. If it is, continue to pursue it. If the position has been filled, mark it as filled. Do not discard this information. You may need it in the future.

Never overlook important leads and information in the newspapers. Don't limit your reading to the classified employment section. Newspapers publish informative articles about companies, industries, executives and other important people. These articles supply you with important facts, names, and leads you can use in your search.

The business section can provide names of top executives who have been recently hired, transferred, promoted or fired. It can also tell you which companies are profitable and unprofitable. It may identify companies that have acquired new contracts and are expanding. These are signs that they may be hiring soon; send in your resumé *before* they advertise these positions.

The lifestyle, trends and editorial sections of the newspaper can also provide valuable information. You'll often find profiles of important people you might approach for help. Make it a daily habit to at least skim through one or more newspapers for leads. Write down important information, clip and save useful articles. Good newspapers keep you informed of the latest trends in the employment market. You might not use this information today, but you may need it next week.

The information in newspapers is usually current. Take advantage of this by immediately putting it to use. It will increase your chances of success a hundredfold by putting you ahead of the crowd. Don't waste valuable information by procrastinating and allowing leads to become outdated and useless.

Another source of important leads and valuable information are magazines, professional trade journals and newsletters. Companies often advertise employment opportunities in them. Even when magazines don't advertise employment opportunities directly, they can provide leads. Companies list phone numbers and important names in their ads. Magazines publish informative articles about companies, industries and their executives. You may discover companies and careers you were previously unaware of. If you see a company that interests you, contact them.

Practically every profession and industry has its own trade journal or newsletter. These publications don't usually show up on your local newsstand. Obtain names of professional trade magazines and newsletters in your field of interest. Review them to get names of companies, executives, and professional organizations. They also list sources for training and places to obtain experience.

Magazines, trade journals and newsletters are often overlooked as sources for employment. Learn which of these publications are useful. Include them as sources for leads and important information; subscribe to them if you can afford to.

Employment Agencies

Employment agencies are businesses that, for a fee, find clients employment or employers. Knowing how to select and use them can make or break your career. Choose agencies as carefully as you would your spouse, doctor, lawyer or business partner.

There are three types of employment agencies:

- employment agencies on retainers
- employment agencies paid by the employer
- employment agencies that charge applicants a fee

If you use employment agencies, understand which type you are using. The first two agencies listed above do not charge applicants. Fees are paid by employers. The agency on a retainer is paid fees in advance by employers for providing various services. They are not paid for specific applicants their clients hire. The second type of agency receives a fee from the employer for each applicant hired.

The third type of agency charges fees to applicants. These fees are charged even if they are unsuccessful in finding them employment. These types of agencies are best avoided. Always ask about an agency's fee arrangement.

How to Find Qualified and Honest Employment Agencies

In any profession there are qualified, honest individuals and ones who are not. No matter what type of employment agency you use, make sure they are reputable. Only work with agencies and individuals that are qualified and reliable.

Make sure agencies are interested in their clients and not just in making money. Many professional recruiters are merely looking for bodies to place anywhere they can for a fee. They don't care whether this decision is in the best interest of the employee and employer or not. These recruiters place candidates in positions even when they know it will be detrimental to their careers. If you are working with an agency or individual and are not satisfied, formally end the relationship. Call them or send a letter saying you want your name removed from their active file.

Ask friends and business associates to recommend reliable agencies. Make sure they used them personally or know others who have. Notice how the agency interviews you. Honest and qualified professional agencies carefully interview and screen their candidates. They do not want to refer bad candidates who would damage their reputation. Interview *them* while they are interviewing you. Ask for the names of companies who recently hired their candidates. Ask where they will be sending you. When possible, discreetly verify the information. Do not feel bad if you do this — after all, agencies will certainly verify your information.

Ask who the agency generally works with. They'll have more clout if they work closely with presidents, CFOs, VPs of human resources or managers who do the actual hiring.

Never allow an agency to pressure you to take a position you are not comfortable with. Usually your feelings are correct. It is critical to work only with agencies and individuals whom you are comfortable with. Good agencies provide professional career counselling to help you in your search. They will not place you in a position merely to gain quick income for themselves. They want long-term relationships with their clients.

Good agencies act as sponsors. They realize that placing candidates in undesirable positions not only hurts the individual but themselves as well. They take the time to help you with interviewing techniques. They honestly and openly discuss your strengths and weaknesses. Their actions are in your best interest, not just theirs. Agencies and individuals who act as sponsors always have repeat business.

Developing Relationships with Agencies

Always give agencies factual information. Never make false statements about your education, skills or experience. Do not make them look bad at an interview. If you do, they will never send you on another interview. They will circulate your name as a bad candidate and other agencies will not represent you.

Always keep your promises. If you promised to do an interview, make sure you do it and are on time. Look your best and project your best image. If you cannot keep the interview or you will be late, call the client and inform them. Also, call the employment agency. If you cannot keep an appointment make sure it is for a valid reason.

Inform employment agencies about what type of position you are seeking during your initial contact. Let them know what you will and will not take. Give them your salary requirements. This will prevent them from wasting their time selling you to a client you are not interested in.

If an agency does set up interviews with clients you are not interested in, refer them to the requirements you provided upon signing with them. Let them know you are not interested in the position.

If you are offered a position and you decide not to accept it, have a valid reason. Declining an offer will result in lost revenue for the agency. Make sure you are not unfairly wasting the agency's time and money. If you do not accept a position, the agency may not want to work with you any longer. If this happens, find another agency.

Employment Agencies' Tricks of the Trade

Employment agencies utilize all types of sources to obtain employment leads. Some agencies obtain leads at the expense of the candidates they are assisting. They get leads from applicants and then use them to place other candidates on their roster. One trick is to contact your present or former employer to offer their services. They know you've left or are about to leave your position, so your "advance information" gives them a chance to send their candidates to apply for your old job.

Another ploy unethical agencies sometimes use is to ask you where you have already applied for positions. They may give the excuse that they do not want to duplicate your work, but what they are really up to is using your leads to try to place other applicants. Sometimes these applicants will end up in direct competition with you for a position.

Agencies may ask for your leads then instruct you not to use them. They will tell you they can better pursue your leads because of their expertise. Often this is not in your best interest. Your leads may be companies that prefer not to work with employment agencies. Having an agency approach them on your behalf will ruin your chances of obtaining the position. And as in the situation above, the agency may use your leads to find positions for other candidates.

Another problem can occur when agencies and employers have disputes over fees. An employer may want to hire you but disagree with the agency's fee. If the agency and company cannot agree about the fee, you will not be offered the position. Of course, the agency won't tell you you lost your chance due to a dispute over its fee.

Employment agencies may ask you to work with them exclusively. They will tell you it is only fair because of their work and effort. This request is *not* fair, and you should never agree to it. Your primary objective is to find employment. Never do anything that would restrict your chances for success. Agencies would not be profitable if they only worked with one candidate. It is common practice in the industry to send several candidates to the same interviews. Since you should not expect agencies to work exclusively with you, they should not expect you to work exclusively with them.

The more you network and circulate your resumé, the greater your chances of securing employment. Do not allow others to sabotage your chances for success. Employment agencies are often helpful in finding you employment, but they are not always successful. Do not depend entirely on them to find you a position.

OTHER SOURCES OF INTERVIEWS

Sometimes we fail to tap sources of employment because we are unaware of them or have misconceptions about their value. Employment opportunities can arise from unexpected places, people and situations. I'll review some of these below, but always be aware that excellent career and employment opportunities can present themselves anytime. They can show up when you are not looking for them. Be prepared to explore the possibilities, to act quickly and to take advantage of them.

Big Is Not Always Better

Some people equate small companies with narrow opportunity and low prestige. This is an unfortunate perception; you do not have to work with large organizations to be successful. In fact, smaller companies can sometimes offer advantages over larger ones. For instance, you often gain exposure more quickly and easily than in larger corporations. You can learn more in smaller companies because they often have you work in different departments and perform multiple functions.

In smaller companies there can be greater opportunities to show your initiative and a faster track to senior-level positions. Even when there are limited positions, the experience you gain is transferable — it will allow you to move into senior-level positions in other companies. The number of new positions in smaller companies is often greater than in larger companies. These are companies with 20 or fewer employees. Two-thirds of all new positions created are within smaller companies. Fewer than 20 percent of these companies have formal personnel departments.

Smaller companies are more flexible. They are expanding while large organizations are downsizing to reduce cost. Smaller companies do not have the bureaucracy often found in larger companies. Many smaller companies have become competitive with larger companies in the area of employee benefits.

Powerful but inexpensive computers and software have allowed small companies to compete with large corporations. Smaller companies can often produce work of equal or superior quality. Smaller companies are not burdened with the high overhead larger competitors incur. They can be more agile and ready to adapt to rapid changes in a market. They can be more exciting places to work.

CD-ROMs

One new powerful source for finding employers, their phone numbers and addresses are business directory phone CD-ROM programs. They allow you to search for companies by name, standard industry code (SIC), state, city and zip code. They list millions of businesses. With your computer you can select an industry and find all the listed businesses within your city, state or nationwide within minutes. You can use this list to call businesses or send resumés.

Libraries

Libraries are excellent sources for leads and other valuable information. They can provide you with directories of associations and businesses. They can give you data on current trends, developments and statistics that are invaluable for employment and career searches. They provide books on every subject from A to Z. You can find books on job banks, developing self confidence, and writing resumés.

If you don't know what career you want, the library lists every career imaginable. Libraries can help you find what you want to do with your life. Libraries subscribe to trade, business and employment magazines. Librarians can show you how to research efficiently. Libraries provide all these services free. Make the most of your library. Learn to use all its resources and let them work for you.

Job Fairs and Clinics

Job fairs can offer important leads but are very competitive. Participating employers receive a large volume of resumés at these events, so you must make a good impression on the people you meet at them. These representatives are usually personnel staff, not the people who do the actual hiring. They code resumés as they receive them. The coding determines if they are passed on for further review or discarded. This is based on the impression you make, your resumé and skills, and how well you fit their profile.

Follow-up is important for leads obtained through job fairs. Ask for business cards. Let contacts know you will call. Follow up with phone calls and thank-you cards. If this does not produce results, list them in your tickle file and call them monthly. Develop company contacts.

Job fairs sometimes offer employment and career clinics, instructional seminars on methods for finding employment or careers. They are worth attending. Many instructors are knowledgeable and can provide you with important leads and tips.

Colleges and Universities

Colleges and universities offer free employment and career placement services. Most of these services are only offered to their students and graduates. Professors and teachers are good sources for references and many of them have excellent contacts in the business world. Many large and small companies give preferential treatment to students and graduates that highly regarded professors have referred. Professors often sit on companies' boards of directors. They are excellent contacts and are recognized in their industry. References from them can guarantee employment.

Business leaders in turn often sit on a school's board of directors. They work closely with professors and college officials. They hire students and graduates school authorities recommend. Learn who has clout at your college or university. Make sure you develop a positive relationship with them. After graduation keep in contact with your school alumni and faculty. Join school-booster programs after graduation. The contacts you make are priceless.

Technology has now made remote interviews possible. Candidates and interviewers can see and speak to each other in real time with the aid of a computer. This has become popular with colleges and universities. All that is required is video conferencing software, a phone and a camera attached to your PC. Applicants can interview with companies anywhere in the world without leaving campus. This also alleviates the concerns of companies who were unwilling to send recruiters to geographically undesirable locations.

Many colleges and universities have created remote interviewing rooms on campus. This service is attracting major companies. Find out if colleges and universities in your area use this technology. If they do, take advantage of it. If they don't, request that they start a remote interview program. Volunteer to help set this program up. It will create great networking opportunities and provide access to companies and prominent individuals who can hire you.

Many companies are also conducting remote interviews off campus. For less than one hundred dollars you can purchase video conferencing software and a camera for your PC and conduct remote interviews from home. Find out which companies conduct remote interviews and let them know you can utilize this technology. You can also indicate on your resumé and letter of introduction you are available for remote interviews.

Outplacement Consulting Firms

Outplacement consulting firms are doing record business. They do not place employees in new positions or careers; rather, they help them develop skills to find them. Companies hire them to place employees whom they've laid off. They teach interviewing techniques, how to write resumés and cover letters, how to obtain leads, and other career-related skills. Be sure to take advantage of these services if offered. If your employer has announced layoffs or plant closures, and does not provide outplacement services, request them. If enough employees request these services, your company may provide them.

Company Bulletin Boards

Companies often post vacant and new positions weekly on on-site bulletin boards for employee review. Ask friends and family members to have a look their company's bulletin boards. They can inform you of positions that match your interests. Contact companies to learn if they post positions. Request a copy of their recent list. If you cannot obtain one, visit the company to review their positions.

Reviewing internal job listings gives you a jump on the general public. Employers usually list positions internally prior to public release.

Whenever you visit companies, look for their job bulletin boards. City, state, and federal agencies post job vacancies in public areas. Make a list of employment bulletin board locations that includes when new openings are posted (every Monday, first of the month, etc.). Ask friends and family members to review their employers' job listing on the day they are posted and inform you of any suitable positions. If you don't have a company contact, do it yourself. When you visit a site use networking techniques described earlier to solicit company employees to do this for you. Remember that companies are not the only employers who list openings on their bulletin boards. Do not overlook schools, colleges and universities. They post large listings for entry-level and experienced positions.

The next section describes how you can check "electronic" bulletin boards without leaving home. While the old paper method is not as effective, it is still a tool that is too valuable to be overlooked. Large numbers of companies do not post their positions on electronic bulletin boards. The old method also provides opportunities to find positions even when you are not actively looking. Seeing the ideal position posted on an employer's bulletin board will entice you to apply for it. It may lead to the start of a successful career.

The Internet

The Internet is the world's largest computer system. It had its origins in the ARPANET, a Department of Defense attempt to create computer networks that would survive military attacks. The Iraqis, at the dismay of the Defense Department, can testify to the effectiveness of the Internet; they used it to maintain military communications after America's devastating bombing of its communications systems during the Gulf War.

Now you must be thinking, What does the Internet have to do with finding employment? Pounding the pavement and scouring through endless newspaper classified sections for openings are not the most effective uses of our time. As indicated in earlier, studies show only 12 percent of jobs are found through newspaper ads; 75 percent of jobs are obtained through networking. Since the Internet is the world's largest network of computers, it brings a new element of technological efficiency to networking. The Internet is the most cost-effective method for job seekers to find employment, develop contacts and access valuable career information. It allows users to apply for hundreds of positions anywhere in the world within hours, without leaving home. There are more employment listings, leads, services and career opportunities on the Internet than in any other location.

Accessing the Internet requires a computer, modem, Web browser, phone line and an Internet account. Internet accounts can cost as little as $15 a month for unlimited usage. The most popular services are America on Line (AOL), CompuServe and Microsoft Network. As well as access to the Internet, these services provide electronic career and employment forums to assist customers in finding employment, information and leads. If you don't own a computer, find friends who will let you use theirs. Libraries and schools also provide members and students with free access to the Internet.

The Internet is available 24 hours a day, seven days a week. It has thousands of Web sites and job banks designed to match job applicants with businesses looking for employees. You can visit a site by typing its unique address, the Universal Resource Locator (URL), in your browser. Netscape and Internet Explorer are the most popular browsers. Browsers are software programs that allow you to access Web sites. You can travel through linked documents from one location to another with a click of your mouse.

Most Internet Web sites are free to the public. Some institutions such as colleges and schools only allow alumni or current students to use their employment services. Some businesses have an "Intranet," an internal Internet that can only be accessed by their employees. Enlist friends who have access to Intranets to search for positions for you.

The good news is that most businesses and state, federal and employment agencies provide employment listings on their Web sites and allow anyone to search for positions by title, category, city and state. Even major newspaper employment classified ads are available on the Internet. Anyone can search for positions by dates, jobs and locations.

Internet users can also immediately apply for positions by uploading or pasting resumés into Web sites, filling out electronic questionnaires and applications (electronic resumés), or submitting resumés by E-mail. Instead of taking days to travel through traditional mail, resumés are received within minutes or hours. When Web sites do not provide these options, they often provide mailing addresses or fax numbers for submitting resumés. Thousands of employers post job openings and allow applicants to apply for them on their Web sites. There are also thousands of Web sites that allow you to post resumés so that they can be accessed by employers. Even professional recruiters have job data bank Web sites for employers and job seekers. Most of these services are free or charge a nominal fee.

As noted in chapter 2, there are advantages to submitting electronic (scannable) resumés. More and more employers are unwilling to manually sort through hundreds or even thousands of resumés in huge data bases. Instead, they use computer software to select resumés from their computer job banks. Sophisticated software such as Resumix goes beyond just searching for key words and phrases. Resumix will also interpret candidates' resumés and match their skills to a position's requirements. Within minutes, it will search through thousands of resumés and select only those that meet the position's criteria. Know the key words, technical jargon and other components employers use in their search for positions in your field. Include them in your resumé. To see an example of Resumix, visit their web site at **www.resumix.com.**

Many computerized resumé databases allow applicants to upload resumés directly into their data files. The rules for computer data base resumés are different from those for printed ones. Paper resumés must be cosmetically appealing to the reader's eye to create interest. They should include different fonts, font sizes, styles, and space. This does not work for computer data base resumés. The preferred format is an ASCII (American Standard Code for Information Interchange) text file. This format allows prospective employers to search, download, read and print resumés no matter what type of word processor they use.

Word processing programs can easily save resumés as ASCII text files. Select your "Save As" feature, then name the file and select file type — ASCII format. When you convert your resumé to an ASCII text file, you lose all special effects (fancy fonts, different font sizes, bold, italic, centering and special characters). Before you submit your ASCII-text resumé to job data banks, review it and correct any errors. It is best to make resumés flush left and keep the file size to a maximum of 5K.

When uploading resumés, list them in the proper job category and with a job title. Indicate your state and if you are willing to relocate. Find out how long resumés remain in the data base so you can re-submit if needed. Resumé services provide instructions for uploading resumés.

Some job data banks do not use resumés. Instead they require candidates to complete applications or questionnaires that they then maintain in their data bases. Many experts foresee on-line searches becoming one of the most effective ways to find employment and fill positions in the future.

E-mail also allows users to send and receive messages at any time. E-mail stands for electronic mail. It can be sent instantly over the Internet. Veteran E-mail users refer to our U.S. postal system as "snail mail" because it takes days or weeks for delivery. E-mail is easy to use and can include sophisticated features such as attached files (your resumé), voice messages, video clips and pictures.

Many businesses prefer and request E-mail resumés because they can respond quickly and easily to them. E-mail also reduces paper clutter. Most recipients request resumés in WordPerfect, Microsoft Word or ASCII format. If you don't know what format the E-mail recipient can read, submit your resumé as an attached ASCII file.

It has become common for large and small companies to have Web sites. They provide job seekers with valuable contacts, business profiles and employment information. The growing trend is for individuals to have Web sites as well. This is an excellent way to expand your networking capabilities and opportunities for employment. Your site can range from one to any number of Web pages. Anyone with an Internet address can create a Web site to promote their resumé, services, skills and unique talents. Web sites can include samples of your work, pictures, audio and video clips, lists of awards and achievements, and references. They provide a means for employers to find and contact you. You can link your Web site to other sites that attract companies and individuals interested in hiring you. Software such as Microsoft FrontPage or Adobe PageMill makes creating a Web site easy. If you prefer, hire a Web page designer to create your Web site for you. Prices range from free to hundreds of dollars.

If you shop around you can find an Internet service provider (ISP) to host your site for less than you think. I found one that provides unlimited access to the Internet and E-mail accounts, and hosts my business Web site and domain name (**www.anthonystith.com**) for about the same cost as basic cable-TV service. A domain name is a unique URL address registered to an individual or company. At present the cost to purchase a domain name is $70 for two years and $35 a year thereafter. Having your own domain name is not only impressive, it creates a recognizable identity. To order your domain name visit **http://www.internic.net**.

The Internet provides access to thousands of different data bases covering virtually any topic. You can research business topics, companies, career opportunities, financial information, products, services and background information on important individuals. These are invaluable research tools to assist you in finding employment and career opportunities. Most of this information is free or available for a small charge.

Don't know how to find information on the Internet? Internet search engines make it easy to find whatever you are looking for. The most popular search engines are Yahoo, Lycos, InfoSeek, Excite and Alta Vista. Search engines allow users to type in key words and search the Internet for related information. You can find company Web sites, job data banks and other helpful information. Internet search features also include the yellow and white pages, ATT 800 directories, E-mail listings, and a *Directory of USA People*.

The Internet also includes news groups and Internet relay chat (IRC), commonly referred to as chat rooms. They cover every imaginable topic. By subscribing to news groups that include "job" in their names, you can obtain thousands of available job listings, with descriptions, company profiles and instructions for applying. Chat rooms allow several users anywhere in the world to communicate simultaneously, like a conference call via the keyboard, for the cost of a local call. Another Internet feature is the ability to have information automatically delivered to your computer. You can actually have job postings delivered directly to your computer daily.

All this should be ample motivation to get wired. Above all, using the Internet makes you stand out because it shows technological expertise that employers desperately need. Computer skills and the ability to research efficiently on the Internet are invaluable in today's competitive employment market. See the Resources section for a list of the best employment and career Web sites.

Book Stores

Browse through the business, employment and career sections of any book store. You will find directories, job bank listings, career aptitude books and other career guidance tools. Larger cities may have book stores specializing in business books — these may have the best selection of career guides.

Book stores tend to have more current material than libraries. Unfortunately, many libraries' budgets have been drastically reduced, and they are unable to purchase new books. Books can be expensive; consider getting together with fellow job hunters and pooling your resources to buy the books you want. If several of you want the same book, arrange a bulk purchase from the store or distributor at a discount.

Don't forget the Internet book stores such as **amazon.com**. They are good places to find books not available at your local book shop.

Multi-Level Marketing Techniques

Multi-level marketing is a sales method whereby a person recruits others to sell for them. This is a way of expanding your distribution of a product or service. You can easily apply this technique to your employment search. Here's how it works:

Identify your strengths and determine how they can benefit employers you would like to work for. Now, list 10 to 25 people you know and the industries they work in. Match them with your skills and experience. Contact these individuals and schedule separate meetings with them. If you can, take them to lunch. Make them feel comfortable. Remember, you want their assistance. Ask them to help you in circulating your resumé at their place of work or anywhere else appropriate. Be polite and professional when you ask them to circulate your resumé. Tell them you will understand if they decline. Never try to force anyone to circulate your resumé.

If they agree to circulate your resumé, give them no more than five copies to distribute for you. Never give individuals a large number of resumés unless they ask for them. This often turns people off and makes them feel like you've given them a part-time job finding you employment. Tell them you will gladly provide additional copies if needed. When people agree to circulate your resumé for you, send them a thank-you note or card.

Now you will see the power of multi-level marketing: If you give five individuals five resumés, they will circulate twenty-five or more resumés. Often people will make additional copies to circulate. Anyone who receives your resumé can send it to someone who will hire you. In this way you stretch out your contacts to a degree you could never achieve on your own. Keep resumés with you always, in your brief case and car. You never know when opportunities will arise.

When you circulate resumés to new contacts, follow these guidelines: Never give resumés to new prospects without first building rapport. If you don't, your resumé will be placed in the nearest trash bin once you are out of sight. Develop techniques to skillfully sway conversations toward finding employment. Master this skill so prospects will solicit your resumé. This shows you've generated interest in yourself and made a good impression.

Sometimes whatever you do, people may still be reluctant to help you. You probably won't want to bother with these people, but someone you have a poor relationship with may be your only source of important contacts. In these cases, try offering a finder's fee. Tell them you'll pay them if you get hired through one of their contacts.

Business Cards

Business cards are inexpensive but powerful networking tools. People tend to throw away and misplace slips of paper with phone numbers, but they usually retain business cards. Your cards may not generate results immediately but will eventually. Business cards help to build bridges for communication. They make it easy for people to contact you.

Try to create a rapport and a positive impression prior to handing out business cards. When you give others your business card, always ask for theirs in return. It shows you are interested in the person you met and gives you a way to keep in contact with them. Keep a card file of all the cards you obtain. You never know when you will need them or their contacts.

If you are unemployed, print personal business cards showing your home phone and fax number, address, E-mail address if you have one, and occupation. This presents a professional image even when you are out of work.

Gatekeepers and Secretaries

When calling businesses for employment or leads, we often have to get past gatekeepers and secretaries. Gatekeepers and secretaries can be allies or formidable foes. You can make them work for you or against you. Once you realize this, working with them is easier.

Gatekeepers are receptionists or those in the department who answer the phone. They may or may not work for the person you are trying to contact. They may have limited knowledge about them. They often just take messages and screen unwanted calls to prevent needless interruptions.

Secretaries, on the other hand, are knowledgeable about their bosses' time and affairs. They often schedule their appointments. They have influence over whom their bosses see and speak with. People who call for employment leads are considered nuisances unless they create an interest or relationship. Even when positions are available, due to the large number of inquiries managers do not have the time nor the desire to speak with every candidate.

To get past gatekeepers and secretaries, and to obtain their assistance, be prepared. Know how to establish rapport and overcome objections before you make your calls. Be polite and respectful to gatekeepers and secretaries. Always smile when you are speaking on the phone; your audience will feel the warmth and friendliness you project. When gatekeepers and secretaries introduce themselves memorize their names and the sound of their voices. Learn the correct pronunciation. Write it down for future reference. Remembering people's names makes them feel respected and important. Politely ask for their name if they do not provide it. Be formal at first — use Mr., Miss, Ms. or Mrs. or whatever the person prefers. Don't address people by their first name unless they ask you to.

Introduce yourself before you ask to speak with the individual you want. If you do not know who it is you want to speak with, ask for assistance. Whenever someone helps you, thank them. Before gatekeepers or secretaries direct your call they will ask the nature of your call. If secretaries decide you are some needless interruption they will prevent you from speaking with the party you want. Often if you inform a secretary you are looking for a job you will receive these types of replies: "Interviews are handled by Human Resources," "There are no openings," "The party is unavailable [or in a meeting, or out of town, or on vacation]." Develop ways to overcome these objections and obstacles.

Use referrals to overcome objections (their friends, mutual friends, important people, organizations, social and business associates). Ask prominent individuals for introductions. If you can't get them to introduce you, ask for permission to use them as a reference. Drop names of prominent people when speaking with secretaries or gatekeepers. Let them know their boss expects your call.

When you have an appointment or your call is expected, objections are eliminated. You could also avoid gatekeepers by setting up appointments outside the work environment; social events are effective ways to obtain leads and interviews.

Before you make a call, write scripts to practice your delivery. Even though you are using scripts you must not sound like you are using them. Never speak in a monotone voice, too fast or too slow. Your scripts must include your introduction and the reason for your call. They must include ways to overcome obstacles and objections. Practice until you are comfortable with them. They should be brief and to the point, but warm and professional.

When you call and are asked the nature of your call, use the script you think will be the most successful. Be prepared for obstacles or objections. One common objection is that their boss is busy. To this you might respond that you only need a few minutes of his or her time. Promise them you will be brief. Many managers do not want to be bothered with individuals asking for employment. If the secretary tells you the boss has no openings, or that Human Resources handles the interviewing, counter with a suggestion you are interested in obtaining information about the industry and the company.

If the secretary says the boss is out of town, in a meeting or on vacation, ask when they will return and the best time to call them. If you are unable to speak with them, try to obtain leads from the secretary. Ask for names and numbers of other department heads who may be helpful. Remember, Human Resources may not always be the best source for leads. They do not hire employees, they only refer candidates to the people who do. Try to contact the people who do the actual hiring. Always focus on your objectives and remember their priority: You want to obtain employment, speak with individuals that can hire you, or develop new leads.

When you speak with secretaries, listen on the phone for anything that can help you. Hearing someone wish the secretary a happy birthday or offer congratulations on a promotion can be used to create rapport. Congratulate them yourself. Send a belated birthday or congratulation card. Always send a thank-you card for their time and help. The next time you speak with them they will be more helpful. Your thoughtfulness will go a long way.

If you hit a brick wall with gatekeepers or secretaries, find out when they go to lunch and call during that time. Try calling early or late. Many managers start work before their secretaries arrive and stay after they leave. Early in the morning or after hours, managers often answer their own phones.

Voice Mail

Modern technology has produced another popular form of gatekeeper. This one is not human so you so cannot win it over by being kind. It is called voice mail.

Voice mail is impersonal. It is not as persuasive as direct phone contact, especially if you are making exploratory phone calls. If you've never had contact with the person you're trying to reach, if you don't know whether positions are available, or if you are not acting on a referral, don't leave a message on voice mail on your first call.

Often voice mail states the party is either on the phone or out of their office. This means a person does answer the phones eventually. Be prepared for voice mail. If you have strong referrals or connections, leave a message on your first call. If not, make several more attempts at getting a live response before you leave a voice message. Your messages should not sound like you were annoyed.

Make voice mail work for you. Use it to display your speaking skills, personality, and intelligence. Use it to drop names and references that create interest. Use scripts that do not sound like scripts. When leaving a message make it clear, intelligent, professional, and friendly. Develop rapport with the voice on the line.

Messages should be brief — no longer than 30 seconds. Motivate prospective employers by giving them time-sensitive incentives to call you. For example, a tax specialist could leave a message like, "I can reduce your company's tax liability by 40 percent if you plan ahead and use my services now."

Never make promises you cannot keep. Think before you speak. Remember, once you've said it you cannot take it back. Effective messages create positive images and make employers want you. Show you are special by being different, but do it in good taste. Also, use voice mail options. They give you the opportunity to speak with someone who can provide information.

Fax Machines

If you are unable to bypass gatekeepers or voice mail, send a letter of introduction by mail or fax. It may be sent to a person who will hire you. Make it brief, to the point, and interesting. Use attention-grabbing fax cover sheets to attract readers. Fax machines are excellent for sending or receiving information quickly. Many companies ask applicants to fax resumés to them.

Some companies provide "fax-on-demand" services. Instead of speaking with operators they request your fax number and immediately fax the requested information back to you. Rather than waiting days or weeks to receive information you can get it in minutes or hours. If you don't receive the information in several hours you can call and inform the party you did not receive it. You can also fax your response within minutes instead of days and gain a big advantage. Having a fax number also presents a professional image.

Today it is standard for computers to be equipped with fax/modem cards. If you own a computer without one, install one. You can also purchase a fax-phone switch that lets you use a single phone line for your phone, fax and modem. It differentiates between tones for voice, fax and modem calls and automatically routes the call to the proper device. This eliminates the expense of installing a second phone line.

Computer fax systems and fax machines have their advantages and disadvantages. Computer systems tend to be cheaper than fax machines, but they are unable to receive faxes when the computer is turned off. Another drawback is you cannot fax paper documents outside your computer unless you have a scanner. If you can afford it, a separate fax machine is a good investment. Currently these machines can cost as little as $100, but cheaper machines use rolls of thermal paper that tends to curl up and fade. They also will not give the best results when transmitting faxes. There are more expensive machines that also function as printers and scanners for your computer and may be a better use of your money. Alternatively, ask permission from a fax machine owner or a faxing service to use their number as your fax number.

Follow-Up

Finally, follow up on new and old employment leads. They can be valuable sources of employment and careers. Successful follow-up has four components:

- follow up opportunities with calls or meetings
- follow up calls and meetings with thank-you cards or confirmation letters
- follow up with calls or meetings to finalize objectives
- follow-up must be timely

Immediate follow-up is the key to success. Follow up on leads while they are hot and before others take advantage of them. Don't hesitate. If you tell someone you will call or send a resumé tomorrow, keep your promise. It shows reliability.

Follow up on cold leads. They can turn into the career you want. Just because you did not get the position yesterday, does not mean they will not hire you today. Things change. People come and go. The person who would not hire you yesterday may have quit, been fired, or transferred. Positions they filled yesterday may be vacant today. A company may have just signed a multi-million-dollar contract and will need to double its staff. You will only find out if you follow up on old prospects.

* * *

You now have numerous ways of finding and approaching a potential employer. Don't rely on one particular method alone to generate interviews. Tailor these techniques to your own purposes and your field. Remember that in some fields formality is important, while others value creativity and originality.

Be organized. Keep a journal of your employment search. Record names of people you have spoken with or sent resumés to (remember also to note the type of resumé you sent). Always have a notepad and pen with you to write down contact names people give you. Have a business card to hand out. You never know when you will meet the person who can give you that one bit of information you need to get the position you want; always be prepared.

Above all, do not give up. Winners never quit. Scientist Louis Pasteur said, "Let me tell you the secret that led me to my goal. My strength lies solely in my tenacity." Tenacity is the conviction to follow up and follow through until you achieve your desired goals.

Chapter 4

Preparing for the Interview

The crowning fortune of a man is to be born to some pursuit which finds him employment and happiness, whether it be to make baskets, or broadswords, or canals, or statues or songs.

—Ralph Waldo Emerson

IF YOU'VE started using the interview-generation techniques described in chapter 3, you should have at least one interview scheduled by now. Congratulations! You're one step closer to getting the position you want.

The interview is your chance to shine. You want to capture your potential employer's interest and show them that you will be an asset to their company or organization. Nobody can do this without careful forethought and preparation. In this chapter you will learn techniques that will help you ace that interview.

TEN STEPS TO PREPARE YOURSELF FOR INTERVIEWS

What you do prior to interviews determines how successful you are during interviews. If you master the following ten steps you will be focused and on the right track to obtaining the career you desire.

1. Recognize Marketable Skills and Assets (Know Thyself)

Identify your marketable skills. Your skills are not just what you've done in the past for pay. Hobbies, volunteer work, interests and experiences are important and useful. They are transferable skills. Take inventory of all your talents, assets, skills, and experiences:

- Write down all your skills.
- Identify skills you do best.
- Identify skills you enjoy doing.
- Rank them in order of enjoyment.

What you do best may not be what you enjoy most. Gear your career toward what you enjoy most. Genuine enthusiasm is the greatest asset you have. Enthusiasm gives you the energy and stamina to overcome obstacles. This is what provides you with pleasure, happiness and satisfaction and makes you look forward to working.

2. Research, Research, and More Research

You should know at least something about what a company does before you send them your resumé. If you are invited for an interview, it's imperative that you find out everything you can about your prospective employer — their history, corporate structure and culture, recent changes, financial situation, and so on. Having this information will help you anticipate the types of questions you will be asked. More important, it will help you ask intelligent questions that will impress the interviewer. Showing you are well informed about the company and its industry inspires confidence.

Where do you find this information? Check out the company's Web site on the Internet. Your city's reference library is another goldmine of data — corporate directories and current and back issues of newspapers, magazines and trade journals are excellent sources of information. Enlist the reference librarian's help. If there is time, call the company or organization and ask for a copy of their annual report. Use your network to find someone who works for the company or did so in the past; politely quiz them about your prospective employer.

3. Do Extra Credit Homework

In school extra credit homework can change C's to A's. In the working world it can change failure into success and unemployment into employment. It can change demeaning jobs into successful careers.

This extra credit homework goes beyond the research you did in step 2 above. Now you extend your research to the whole industry your prospective employer is involved in. Find out the current and future trends. Know what employers need and the qualifications they seek. There is often a difference between what an employer needs and what an employer seeks in employees. Sometimes employers do not know what they need. If you show employers you can fulfill important needs they were unaware of, you gain a tremendous advantage during your interview. Match your skills, experience and training to employers' needs.

During the interview, your goal is to speak with authority and show you are knowledgeable. When speaking about your field express positive ideas and comments and make valuable recommendations. Know the names of the leaders and innovators of these industries. Learn the art of name dropping but do it gracefully. It's impressive if you know or have met important people in your field. It doesn't matter if it was just a brief encounter — the interviewer does not know that. If you can use important individuals as references, it enhances the possibility of being hired.

One final comment about extra credit homework: Always give something extra. Show this quality in your work, in your attitude and in interviews. Companies dream about employees who are willing to go the extra mile. Employers know these employees make them successful. Most employees lack this quality. When you display this attitude, you place yourself above the crowd. This one quality will make employers hire you.

4. Create a "Sales Presentation" for Yourself

One of the erroneous perceptions many African Americans, other minorities, and women tend to have of the working world is that degrees, diplomas and certificates are all that are required for a successful career. There are historical reasons for this misconception. Minorities and women were long prevented from getting the training needed to enter certain fields. And in that old Catch-22, they were then told they could not enter certain fields because they did not have the training. Today, minorities and women are better educated than ever before — in some areas they are even surpassing white males in their levels of qualification. This is an important and remarkable achievement.

Saying degrees and diplomas do not matter may be a bit of an overstatement. However, employers now take education and formal training as a given. You will be knocked out of contention if you lack the right degree or diploma, but that piece of paper in itself will not be enough to land you a job.

What does this mean for your interview? In today's multimedia world, it is not enough to merely *tell* a potential employer what you have to offer them, you've got to *show* them. The interviewer already will be aware of your qualifications and work experience from your resumé. Now they'll want tangible evidence of your abilities. Part of this lies in your appearance and manner at the interview, how you speak and respond to questions.

The other part is in how you sell yourself. You need to prepare a sales presentation (pitch) for yourself. Don't just talk about your accomplishments and abilities; instead, find ways of illustrating them visually. For instance, if you devised a marketing approach that boosted sales, show it with a graph. If you gave a speech at a conference, have a photo of the occasion. There are different ways of displaying these materials. A low-tech method is to have a binder that converts to an easel. You can set it up for display and use it in a flip-chart manner. You could create a color slide presentation using presentation software such as PowerPoint and show it on a note-book PC during the interview. If you don't have a notebook PC, print your color presentation on paper. You can get really elaborate with a multimedia presentation on CD-ROM.

The method you choose for making your presentation depends on you and what the position requires. The presentation itself can be a way of showing your adeptness with a required software program or your creativity. Whatever technique you decide to use, your sales presentation must be specific and brief. It must be something inter-viewers and companies find interesting and exciting. It must be well thought out and properly prepared. Sales presentations must be vivid, descriptive and colorful. They must be clear and easy to understand. Include important information you obtained during your research.

Determine what you have to offer companies prior to interviews. Prepare your sales presentation well. It must show what you have to offer and how you can help prospective employers reach their goals. Make sure your presentation fits the style and flavor of the compa-nies or individuals you meet. Have different versions of your sales presentation to fit the needs of different employers.

Know your presentation forward and backward. Consider it a show the interviewer has paid to see. Be professional. Don't fumble around trying to find materials or be forced to say you've forgotten something — it shows you are not organized. You never want to give this impression to interviewers.

Notice how interviewers react to your presentation and adapt to their responses. Even well-made plans encounter unforeseen prob-lems. Be versatile and adapt your sales presentation to whatever sit-uation occurs. To be successful you must be flexible. Don't lose your concentration or confidence when you have to cope with unforeseen situations. Successful people use these situations to their advantage and earn extra points with interviewers by showing they can think on their feet.

5. Rehearse Interviews in Advance

After you complete the steps above, rehearse two or three thirty-minute interviews with someone who is familiar with your career. Each practice interview should be on a different day. Ask a third qualified person to observe and critique each interview.

Conduct these practice interviews as if it they were the real thing. Bring copies of your resumé and other materials you would bring to a real interview. This includes your briefcase, pens, paper, past work, letters of recommendation, sales proposals, awards, and so on. Dress as you would for interviews. If you wear suits to interviews, wear one for your practice session. Prepare for your practice interview as you would for a real one. This includes shaving, showering, getting a hair cut or having your hair done.

During the practice session, the interviewer and observer should not make any verbal review comments. All review comments should only be made after the practice interview is over. Ask them to write down their comments as you are doing the interview. List tough questions that potential interviewers will ask. Before you start the interview, ask the practice interviewer to ask these questions. Ask the interviewer to be as realistic as possible. Let the interviewer know you do not want them to go easy on you. Here are possible tough questions and issues you may have to deal with during interviews:

- Bad references
- Why were you fired?
- Reasons for job hopping
- Inexperience
- Employment gaps on your resumé
- Lack of education
- Reason for leaving former position

Develop appropriate answers to tough questions prior to interviews. Your answers are good if they show you in a positive light. Answer them calmly and confidently. Never be unprepared. Use common sense and good judgment when answering questions. Answers must never be offensive or inappropriate. Be very careful in your use of humor — people have widely varying tastes.

Be prepared to answer common questions interviewers ask. Most applicants fail to prepare themselves to answer common questions such as, What are your strengths, weaknesses? What can you do to help this company? Interviewers always ask applicants to tell them about themselves. Be comfortable talking about yourself. There is nothing wrong with saying you are not perfect and made mistakes in the past. It is fine if you can show you learned valuable lessons from past mistakes. Show how these lessons can benefit your new employer. No one is perfect. If you try to come across as perfect, interviewers will be suspicious of you.

After the practice interview, have the interviewer and observer list areas for improvement. Make audio tapes of practice interviews. Listen to your tone of voice, expressions and how you speak. Do you speak clearly, too soft or too loud? Do you pause too long or speak too quickly? Does your voice crack, do you sound nervous? Do you use inappropriate phrases? Identify any improvement areas.

If possible, use a camcorder to videotape practice interviews. It is the most effective way to develop powerful interviewing skills. Review your expressions and mannerisms to eliminate negative habits. Is your body consistent with your speech? Notice facial expressions, hand and body movements. Do you display nervous habits?

Observing your actions during practice interviews may reveal why you were not hired in the past. Your mannerisms may show fear, nervousness, frustration, impatience or a lack of confidence. Videotapes show if you appear too eager or too desperate. You will also learn how to react under various situations during interviews.

Your practice interviewer and observer must grade you and let you know if you were prepared. Develop a plan to improve any areas of weakness. One technique is to practice speaking in front of a large mirror. Practice making facial expressions. Is your smile natural or is it phony? Learn to look confident, interested and sympathetic. Use expressions that show honesty and sincerity. Be comfortable using them so that you create the impression you desire.

Once you have corrected any deficiencies, tape your interview again. Compare it with the first taped interview. Repeat this process until you become confident and master the art of interviewing.

6. Prepare in Advance for the Scheduled Interview

Use an appointment book to keep track of interviews and appointments. Using an appointment book prevents scheduling conflicts and keeps you organized. Write down important information — contact names, addresses and phone numbers. Putting this information in your appointment book also allows you to keep track of dates and important information. Also, remember that if you are on unemployment benefits you may be required to give evidence of your employment search. It makes your search easier when you keep good records.

Develop a checklist of things you must do to prepare for your interviews. Several days prior to interviews review your checklist. It will identify potential problems in advance. Reviewing it well in advance gives you a chance to correct potential problems before they occur. Once you develop your checklist, make copies of it to use for each interview. Below are just a few items you need to check off prior to interviews. Add any other items you need.

__ Phone numbers	__ Resumé copies
__ Interview time	__ Sales presentation materials
__ Salary history	__ Hair cut
__ Reference information	__ Pen and paper
__ Clean clothes	__ Organized briefcase

__ Contact names   __ Address and date cards

__ Directions to interview   __ Referral names

__ Pre-completed job application   __ Interview homework

__ Time to leave for interview   __ Shine shoes

Earlier I explained the usefulness of having a pre-completed application in your briefcase. When you are asked to fill out an application at interviews, just pull out your pre-completed job application and you have all the information at your fingertips. You will not have to look for or try to remember vital information. You will never have to tell potential employers you must call them back after you find missing information.

Obtain permission in advance for references you plan to use. If the references agree, give them a three-by-five card to complete. Ask them to print or type their name, address and a phone number where they can be reached during regular business hours. If they fail to complete the card do not use them. Ask about 10 people to do this. You'll need at least three good references. Select individuals who know you, are comfortable with you, and are reliable.

7. Emphasize What You Can Do for the Employer

John Fitzgerald Kennedy inspired a nation when he said, "Ask not what your country can do for you, ask what you can do for your country." You can use this approach to inspire, impress and win over interviewers. Employers are not interested in what *they* can do for *you*; they want to know what *you* can do for *them*. This should be the primary focus of your interview. Be prepared to show how you can assist employers to achieve their desired goals. Employers are interested in employees who

- can increase profits (increase productivity and reduce costs)

- can increase market share
- can implement new technology
- can improve morale and competitiveness
- can demonstrate leadership qualities and have the ability to instill them in others
- can provide beneficial training to other employees
- have a positive mental attitude
- are altruistic
- are able to make things happen
- are willing and eager to learn
- have high energy levels
- solve problems and enjoy challenges
- have specialized skills

Think of ways to display as many as these qualities as possible during interviews — your sales presentation may be a good opportunity for this. These skills and qualities are what employers want and are the reasons they hire candidates.

8. Learn to Relax

It's natural to be nervous about interviews. After all, interviews are usually make-or-break situations — often they're your one and only chance to sell yourself to an employer. You don't want to blow it. One tip for dealing with nervousness is to recognize that it is natural; every interviewee is nervous to some degree. Adequate preparation will decrease nervousness. Following the interview-preparation steps above will go a long way toward calming you down.

Appearing relaxed and being at ease with your interviewer inspires confidence. It's another way of making a good impression. Practice relaxation exercises, such as taking long, slow, deep breaths, and slowly tightening, then relaxing your muscles. If nervousness is part of your personality, look into classes on relaxation, meditation and reducing stress. Find out what techniques work for you and put them into action prior to that big interview. By getting your body to relax, your mind will follow.

Some people find repeating an "affirmation" helps them relax and build up their confidence. On the way to the interview, repeat a positive phrase, such as "I'm the best candidate for this job," over and over in your mind. If nothing else, it should block out any fears and doubtful thoughts that may be intruding into your head.

9. Make Good Use of Your Waiting Time

Arrive 15 minutes or so before your appointment. You may not relish the prospect of sitting idle in the waiting area, but in fact you won't be sitting idle. Your waiting time is another chance to prepare for the interview and make a good impression. For one thing, your interviewer may appreciate being able to start the interview earlier than planned. Score one point for you! Chances are, though, that you will have to wait until the appointed time. This gives you time to hang up your coat, check yourself in the mirror, and go to the restroom if necessary.

If the receptionist or assistant is the chatty type, engage him or her in light conversation. You might pick up some useful information about the company or your interviewer's state of mind. Be on your guard, though — some employers ask for their receptionist's or secretary's opinion of a prospective employee, so make sure you leave a good impression. One interviewee was sitting waiting to be interviewed when he saw that the secretary was having trouble with her fax machine. The interviewee had a lot of experience with ornery fax machines, so he offered to take a look at it for her. He was able to quickly fix the problem, thus both demonstrating his resourcefulness and impressing a potentially influential employee.

Another waiting room activity is to have a look at any corporate communications material on display. If none is in view, ask the receptionist for a brochure or any other materials available. Observe your surroundings and the attitudes of employees. It can help you gauge the tone of the company and what level of formality to adopt during the interview. Practice your relaxation techniques.

10. Establish Rapport During the Interview

Be prepared to find common interests to develop relationships with interviewers. Once you enter the interviewer's office, take the time to observe the office, its contents and the interviewer. You can quickly pick up valuable information. I like to use the movie *The Seven Per-Cent Solution* as an example. It is a movie about Sherlock Holmes. In one scene, Holmes reveals intimate and personal details about Sigmund Freud immediately upon entering his study, without any prior knowledge of him.

Within seconds, Holmes could tell that Freud was Jewish but studied other religions, that he was Hungarian and a brilliant physician, was married and had a young son. Holmes also knew that Freud had recently been reading Shakespeare. He was also able to determine that Freud rarely allowed anyone into his private study. Holmes could tell that Freud was a man of honor and had recently severed relationships with his former medical affiliations. Holmes concluded the reason was a possible disagreement they had had with Freud over a new radical theory he had developed.

Sherlock Holmes could tell all this from observations he made as he walked through Freud's study. He could tell Freud was Jewish because of the Hebrew Bible and Talmud on his desk. Holmes also noticed the King James Bible, Book of Mormon and the Koran across the room in Freud's bookcase. Because these books were not kept close to him and because of what Freud kept on his desk (Hebrew Bible, Talmud), he concluded these books were not of his religious faith. Holmes surmised these books were for scholarly purposes.

Holmes could tell Freud was Hungarian by carefully listening to his accent. He could tell he was a brilliant physician because he had volumes of French medical text books in his book cases. This suggested Freud studied in Paris and was able to learn and master the complex science of medicine in a foreign language. He knew Freud was a doctor because he was introduced as such.

Holmes knew Freud did not allow anyone in his private study because it was in need of dusting; the rest of the house was immaculately kept by his housekeeper. He knew he was married because of the wedding ring on his finger. He was also able to tell he had a small son because he observed a small toy soldier on the floor.

Holmes noted one wall of Freud's private study was partially filled with degrees and awards. There were also many outlines of degrees or awards that had recently been removed from the walls. Holmes concluded Freud had disagreed with the established medical profession and no longer associated with them. He determined Freud was a man of honor, for no one except himself would know that he had taken the plaques down. Holmes knew this since it was Freud's private office, to which outsiders were rarely allowed entry. Holmes also knew that Freud had been recently reading Shakespeare because a book of his writings was left open to the page where Freud had stopped reading. The book was on his desk so he could quickly return to it.

Of course, no one expects us to be as observant as the fictitious Sherlock Holmes, but we all can learn a great deal from this example. Successful people take the time to learn as much as possible about the people they meet. They look for information anywhere they can find it. They use it to empower themselves. If we put forth a little effort, we can learn much about interviewers by observing them and their offices. We can learn a great deal by observing awards, degrees, pictures, symbols, decor and people they associate with. Make use of your time as you wait for the interview to begin. Be observant. Use information to build a rapport and create interest in yourself. Use the Sherlock Holmes approach to ensure the success of your interviews.

* * *

If you follow the ten steps above, you will be all set for your interview. Keep in mind that the interview is not a one-way street. Just as the company is interviewing you, you should be interviewing the company. As you do your preparatory research, you may decide that the company or organization is not a place you want to work. If so, go to the interview anyway. If your research has raised troubling issues, tactfully ask the interviewer about them. They may provide reasonable explanations that will eliminate any concerns. If there are problems in the company, maybe you can offer solutions.

Remember that an interview should be a positive experience whether you are hired or not. It is a chance to sell yourself to the employer. If they decide you are not appropriate for the present position, they may consider you for future openings. It can also be a rehearsal for future interviews. If the interview does not go well, learn from it and use it to be better prepared next time.

Chapter 5

The Art of Interviewing

The employer generally gets the employees he deserves.
—WALTER GILBEY

It is no good to know more unless we do more with what we already know.
—AUTHOR UNKNOWN

THE INTERVIEW is your big chance to sell yourself to an employer. Your resumé may get you in the door, but it's the interview that determines whether you get the position.

Some people find that they often make it as far as the interview stage, but never get past it. If you're one of them, the techniques in this chapter, combined with the preparations described in chapter 4, will help you overcome this stumbling block. Many of these techniques are not only useful for interviews but also for any situation where you wish to make a positive impression on people and influence their decisions.

However, no matter what we do, the reality of life is that we will not be offered every position we seek. In fact, the odds are we will be rejected more times than we receive offers. Before we review the do's and don'ts of interviewing, we must look at another element of the interviewing process. To be a good interviewee you must be able to handle rejection.

Coping with Rejection

Rejection is a major problem for most people. We frequently equate our self-worth with our most recent success. If we do not succeed in obtaining a position we hoped for, we lose our self-esteem. The more times we are rejected, the more self-esteem we lose. This can continue until we lose all our self-esteem. If we allow this to happen, we will become poor interviewees and will never obtain the positions we want.

Don't lose your self-esteem when you are turned down for positions you want. It's okay to feel disappointed; feeling bad about yourself is *not* okay. There are many reasons why candidates are not chosen to fill positions. Some relate to what the candidate did or failed to do during the interview; some have to do with the interviewers' own agendas, beliefs and prejudices. In the case of the former, there is much you can do to improve your interviewing skills, as we will discuss below.

As for the latter, sometimes you simply cannot overcome these obstacles. An interviewer with very strong prejudices will be blind to all you have to offer to them and the employer. People may take a disliking to you because of your race, gender, or ethnic background. They may have a nepotistic agenda — they have a friend in mind for a position and are merely going through the motions of interviewing.

In these cases, it is probably better that you were not hired. Working for or with such people can be a nightmare and even professional suicide. For example, one woman was hired for a position after being interviewed by a panel of people including the person who would be her supervisor. This supervisor had wanted to hire a friend for the position but was overruled by the others on the panel. Consequently, when the woman started her new job, her supervisor did everything he could to make her look bad in hopes of getting her fired. Obviously, this type of situation makes for a very unpleasant work atmosphere. Likewise, if you are hired merely to fill some kind of quota rather than for your abilities, your co-workers may resent you and sabotage your work.

It helps to remember that rejection is sometimes for the better in the long run. You can probably think of situations where you were rejected for a position, only to be hired for a better one a few weeks later. Also, if you've made a good impression, the employer may keep you in mind for future positions that open up. Always follow up after interviews if the employer doesn't contact you within a couple weeks. Be polite and positive even if you feel you are out of contention for the position. One candidate ruined her chances for being hired by saying in her follow-up call, "I guess you aren't interested in hiring me." In fact, no decision had yet been made, but this comment resulted in her removal from the list of potential hires.

It's also useful to view each interview as an opportunity for self-improvement, whatever the outcome. If you are turned down for a position after an interview, ask why. You may get advice on skills you need to work on. Analyze the interview yourself — did some questions catch you off-guard? Could you have given better responses? Rather than feel sorry for yourself, figure out why you were rejected and work to improve your weak areas.

It is essential that you remain objective about rejection and not allow it to zap your self esteem. The most important quality to project during an interview is self confidence. If you don't believe you are the best person for the position, the interviewer won't either. Be prepared to interview, interview, interview to obtain the position you desire. Having a solid career plan and specific goals in mind will help you get through this process.

As I mentioned above, there are two general reasons candidates get rejected for positions. I've already discussed one — prejudices of the interviewer. The other is something the candidate did or didn't do during the interview. These deficiencies usually fall into one of two categories: failure to show an ability to do the job, and failure to establish a rapport with the interviewer. The techniques below will address these problems and help you master the art of interviewing.

Sell Yourself and Your Abilities

If you are in the habit of looking for jobs, you'll find it is not an effective way to obtain employment or a career. Instead, learn to sell yourself and your ideas, skills, experience, talents, energy, enthusiasm, personality, and education to interviewers. There is a major difference between candidates who simply look for jobs and candidates who sell themselves to employers. Individuals who sell themselves create positions and careers even when employers are not hiring. Applicants who effectively sell themselves and their abilities have greater success at being hired.

The best way of selling yourself is by making interviewers see you differently from candidates who merely look for jobs. Create a desire in the interviewer to see you, even when positions are not available. Persuade employers that if they hire you it will improve the financial position of their company. Show that if they do not hire you the company will lose something it needs. To do this you must know what the company needs to be competitive and successful. Show interviewers you can provide unique services.

The ability to sell yourself is one of the most important skills needed to obtain the position or career you desire. As explained in chapter 4, your interview must be a sales presentation. You'll gain an advantage if you can inform interviewers of new ideas, services, skills and products that will enhance their companies. It is even more effective if they were not previously aware of them.

Interviews must be informative, interesting and exciting.Use them to showcase your skills, accomplishments and strong points. Convey your messages in brief and clear statements; long-winded statements and answers are boring. Answers and statements should be no longer than one to two minutes. If interviewers want more information, they will ask you for additional details or clarification. Interviewers appreciate clear and precise responses. The practice-interview exercises covered in chapter 4 teach these techniques.

Prior to interviews, find out how much time you will be given. Interviews may range from 15 minutes to several hours in length depending on the position. You can have the best sales presentation in the world, but it becomes ineffective if you get cut off in the middle of it. During practice-interview sessions, learn to complete your sales presentation in the time allotted. Have extended and abbreviated versions to fit all situations. Know how to handle unforeseen situations during interviews. Be flexible and observant. Notice interviewers' likes and dislikes. Steer interviews toward interviewers' interests, not yours. Always strive to present yourself in a positive way.

Present Yourself with Confidence

How you project yourself determines the confidence you inspire. Ultimately, it's not how much you know or don't know. It's not how you dress or how you look. It's not whether you are big or small, fat or skinny. Your confidence is determined by how you feel about yourself. Your inner presence determines whether you project confidence, fear or anxiety.

This inner presence affects how you think, act and move. It is based on your beliefs and your focus. It also is determined by your self-talk and experiences. Your self-talk is what you say to yourself. See yourself in a positive light whatever your situation. This gives you power and confidence. Never focus your thoughts and energies on negative situations. Instead, focus on thoughts that empower you. For example, if you are interviewing and your self-talk is negative, change it. Let's review some kinds of negative self-talk we use that poisons our minds:

- I will make a fool of myself
- I lack experience
- I am not smart
- I am not successful
- I look bad
- No one likes me
- I will never get this position
- I am no good
- I won't be hired because I am black, a minority, or a woman

Henry Ford said, "If we think it's true or if we think it's false, whatever we believe will come true." Learn to remove powerless thoughts from your mind and replace them with the following empowering ones:

- I will create a positive image
- I am a perfect match
- My abilities/talent will prevail
- I will be successful
- I look fine
- I will be hired
- Being black, a minority or a women is not a barrier

If, during an interview, you find yourself thinking negative thoughts, immediately replace them with positive ones. Merely trying *not* to think negative is neither effective nor advisable. This results in you concentrating on not thinking about negative thoughts, which causes you to think about them. Instead, concentrate on filling your mind with empowering thoughts. They will remove negative thoughts from your mind.

Positive thoughts create positive and empowering self-talk within yourself. When you develop positive self-talk, you create an optimistic and powerful inner presence. This positive inner presence generates confidence within and without. Interviewers will not only notice it but feel it as well.

Don't confuse positive thinking with dismissing or ignoring legitimate problems. Instead, use it to generate solutions to those problems. Once you develop solutions and take positive action, you will be able to overcome problems. Often problems only exist in our minds. They originate in false assumptions that we arrived at through fear or ignorance. Unfortunately, once we believe them they become real to us.

Learn to recognize the difference between real and imaginary problems. It is a positive use of time and energy to work to overcome problems that are harmful to us. It is a waste of time and energy to try to resolve imaginary problems. To see the difference between real and imaginary problems, review situations from all angles and not just from a narrow viewpoint. We tend to focus on a single negative element of a problem. We overlook the positive benefits relating to the same so-called problem. If we focus solely on our lack of experience, for example, we fail to see related skills, training and experience we possess or ways to obtain what we need. Situations we see as problems can become opportunities once we solve them.

There will be times where you don't feel well, confident or happy. This can and will happen on days interviews are scheduled. How do we put our best foot forward on days such as these? By learning how to control our thoughts, regardless of how we feel. Successful people have the ability to maintain positive attitudes even when they don't feel well or experience unpleasant circumstances. They do this by focusing on the future and ways to enhance their lives. This allows them to smile and project positive images during difficult times. They create genuine feelings of happiness, humor, confidence, interest, and good will within themselves.

Speak with Power

Exhibit confidence through your speech by your selection of words, tone, and rate of speech. Use words that show you are capable and exhibit confidence. Do not try to impress people with large or complicated words. They are often turnoffs or confusing to listeners. Your choice of words should suit the audience or business you are addressing. They help persuade interviewers to hire you.

Know, understand and use important buzz words and phrases. Buzz words are accepted words, acronyms and phrases commonly used in a particular industry. They show familiarity with the industry and the ability to communicate with others in a particular field. They impress listeners and build rapport.

Carefully distinguish accepted buzz words, acronyms and phrases from offensive slang. Know when buzz words are acceptable. For instance, buzz words that are acceptable in the medical field are not appropriate in the accounting and finance industry. Your words and manner of speech must show you are familiar, competent, and comfortable with the information you are discussing. Your conversation must be easy to understand and create interest in your audience.

Your tone of speech must vary. Never speak in a monotonous voice. Speaking in a monotone is boring and will lose your audience's interest. It will not generate excitement, persuade listeners, show control or confidence. Your voice tone must show enthusiasm and sincerity about your topic. The proper tone of voice makes the speaker believable and persuasive.

Express a wide range of emotions in your voice. Timing is critical when expressing emotions. Never overreact to insignificant issues or act bored about critical issues. Be natural when you speak. Don't exaggerate or understate your emotions. Failing to express appropriate emotions makes your audience think you are insincere. If you don't act interested, your listeners will not be interested.

Be generous with your smile. Express a smile in your voice. It will make your listeners feel at ease. Make a sincere and friendly smile a permanent part of your personality. It is a powerful tool. It not only makes listeners feel comfortable, it makes the speaker feel good. Studies in 1988 at the School of Medicine at the University of California, in San Francisco, showed that our facial muscles are directly related to the limbic system in our brain. Our limbic system is a two-way process. If we think positive thoughts, it is normal to smile. Positive thoughts cause us to smile without any conscious thought or effort. Smiling helps us feel good about ourselves. When we smile, chemical reactions take place in our brains that cause us to think positive thoughts. Our smile is a conditioned reflex. It allows speakers and their audience to feel more at ease, even when they are not meeting under the most favorable conditions.

The rate of speed at which we speak is important. It should not be too slow. This shows you are not sure, lack confidence. Speaking slowly also indicates you are not interested in your topic. People lose interest if you speak too slowly. Speaking too fast also shows a lack of confidence. It's an indication we are nervous and rushing to finish. When we speak too fast, we are unable to emphasize important points, and absorbing what the speaker is saying is difficult. Most listeners will be unable to follow and will stop listening.

When you speak too fast, you also lose the benefit of pausing when you speak. Proper pauses allow your listeners to think about what you just said and improves their retention of what they just heard. It is also helpful if your audience is taking notes.

Use the proper words, tone and rate of speech to get your point across. It will keep your audience's attention. Remember that it takes practice to master the art of speaking. Here's an exercise to learn to create the feeling you want within yourself. Practice speaking as different characters. Feel how a bull dog, a chicken and a confident person might speak. Emulate them in your practice dialog. Practice speaking in a way that projects the image you desire to create. Once you create this feeling in yourself, it shows when you speak.

Success is often determined not by what we say, but by how we say it. When you say your name, smile confidently. Speak in a positive, powerful, friendly and confident manner. Allow your smile to generate warmth inside and out. It will generate warmth in others. Feel your words and let them excite you as you speak. Select a thought (a theme) that creates happiness and confidence in you and your audience.

Use improvisation when you speak. Practice speaking in gibberish and create different moods and emotions. It is an excellent way to learn how to create feelings that are not related to what you are saying. This exercise teaches you to control your mental state. Learn how to use negatives as positive reinforcements. If you fear being judged by others when you speak, then judge *them* when you speak. Do this in a fun way. It should never be done seriously. Instead of being the victim, allow yourself to become the perpetrator in your mind. When you think of yourself as the perpetrator, it becomes difficult to become nervous. When you play this game, do not allow it to affect your outward appearance negatively.

Neurolinguistic Programming (NLP)

A powerful technique has been developed to improve the way we communicate with others. It's called Neurolinguistic Programming (NLP), a highly effective method of communicating. I once heard a speaker give an excellent definition of NLP: "The meaning of our communication is the response we get." If you are not getting the response you want, change what you are doing. NLP involves identifying an individual's preferred method of communication, then responding in that preferred mode of communication. Use the NLP techniques described below to create a bond between you and your audience.

Three of our five senses — sight, sound, and touch — are used as our primary modes of communication. Each of us has a dominant (preferred) mode. We respond more favorably to others who communicate in our preferred mode. When speakers determine their listener's dominant mode of communication and respond in kind, it creates rapport, an atmosphere of mutual trust and harmony.

Use the power of rapport-building to communicate effectively and improve your relationships with interviewers and other important people. Once rapport is created, it's easier to relate ideas and wishes to others. Listeners become more receptive to speakers.

Three methods can be used to quickly determine someone's preferred mode of communication. Studies show people's dominant modes of communication are as follows:

- 60% prefer Visual communication
- 25% prefer Kinesthetic communication
- 15% prefer Auditory communication

First Method — Listen to the Speaker

Listen carefully to interviewers. Determine their preferred mode of communication by their choice of words, especially their verbs. Visual people communicate by seeing pictures in their minds. They speak in terms of seeing — "I see," "I get the picture," "That's clear to me," "I look forward to that." The best way to develop rapport with these people is by visual reinforcement. Use descriptive words to communicate with them. Write things down for them. If you are explaining something, use written instructions. Visual communicators prefer letters and cards to hearing words. They learn by seeing what you are saying. Show them your work, charts and diagrams.

Kinesthetic people communicate by *feeling* what they say. They speak in terms of, "What are your feelings on this matter?" "Will this make you feel better?" "Are you comfortable with this?" The best ways to develop rapport with kinesthetic people are emotional and physical reinforcements. They learn best by doing, and prefer physical signs of affection. They pat people on the back and touch people's shoulders. Use discretion when using these reinforcements. They must be in good taste and not misleading.

Auditory people communicate by hearing. They speak in terms of, "I hear what you're saying," "It sounds like ...", "That clicks," "That sounds familiar." The best way to develop rapport with them is through audio reinforcement. They prefer hearing words instead of seeing letters or documents. They learn best by hearing.

Tailor your responses to the type of people you are talking with. You will not build rapport if you try to communicate with a visual person through auditory responses. When asking questions, match that person's preference. Respond with visual questions if you are speaking to a visual person: "How do you see this working? Can you picture this?" If you are speaking with an auditory person respond by saying things like, "How does this sound to you?"

Second Method — Ask Questions

Asking the right questions can reveal a person's preferred mode of communication. It is not always easy with unfamiliar people. Be careful with your questions — interviewers may feel you are invading their privacy and being offensive. You do not want to do this during interviews. Prior to interviews, master this technique during practice sessions. The sooner we learn the interviewer's preferred mode of communication the faster we can create rapport. Ask neutral questions. They are not personal, sensitive or offensive. Ask questions such as

- What employee qualities are important to you?
- What skills and abilities do you require in an employee?
- What's a typical good day like in the office?
- What's a typical bad day like in the office?

Neutral questions provide insight into interviewers' preferred modes of communication. Answers to your questions can be used to understand interviewers and create rapport.

Do not prejudice interviewers' responses by asking leading questions. It can cause interviewers to respond in the mode of the question and not their preferred mode of communication. "What do you see as important qualities in employees? What qualities do you feel are important in employees? What important qualities in employees make you hear bells and whistles?" All three of these questions are leading because of the words "see," "feel," and "bells and whistles." Asking interviewers questions in your own preferred mode of communication encourages misleading responses. They will reduce opportunities to create rapport.

Third Method — Observe Eye Movement

They say the eyes are the mirrors of the soul. They are also excellent indicators of our preferred mode of communication. By watching and interpreting eye movement, we can determine a speaker's preferred mode of communication.

Scientific studies have determined there is a distinct correlation between our brain, our thinking patterns and eye movement. By properly observing and interpreting eye movement we can determine a person's preferred mode of communication. The rules for interpreting eye movement are simple:

Visual modes see real and imaginary pictures. When a person's eyes look upward and to the left they are visualizing pictures in their mind. This mental picture is based on experiences. For example, if they were talking about a rose, they would see the rose in their mind as they are speaking. This is the most common response. When their eyes look upward and to the right they are creating imaginary pictures in their mind.

Audio modes recall familiar sounds, create new ones and practice self-talk. When a person's eyes look to the left and their eyes are on a level plane they are hearing sounds that are familiar to them. An example would be hearing a favorite song. When their eyes look to the right on a level plane they are creating abstract sounds they've never actually heard. An example would be imagining how the music of love sounds. When their eyes look down and to the left they are having internal conversations. An example would be when they mentally discuss the pros and cons of a proposal prior to making a decision.

Kinesthetic modes feel emotionally and physically. When a person's eyes look downward and to the right they are getting in touch with their emotions and feelings. For example, if they are discussing the weather they start to feel the cold wind in their face, or the hot rays of the sun on their back.

Note that these phenomena only work with right-handed people. With left-handed people, the left and right eye movements are reversed. The upward and downward movements are not affected by being right- or left-handed.

When using this eye technique, do not affect the individual's response by asking leading questions like, "How do you feel? Do you see the picture? Do you hear my point?" Questions like these can affect the listener's eye response. A visual person will respond with an audio eye movement when asked audio questions.

It takes practice to correctly interpret eye movement and to respond in the preferred modes of speech. If you practice and master these skills, they become second nature to you. These techniques are so powerful that even when your answers are not the best ones, they still create rapport.

Speaking and Body Language Skills

Most of us rely on our speaking skills alone to impress and persuade others, and it is essential that we speak properly and effectively. We must know how to properly express and communicate our feelings through words. This includes the most effective use of words to convey our message. We need a good vocabulary. Good speaking skills include proper diction and grammar. The greater our speaking skills, the more we empower ourselves.

It is important to master speaking skills, but we must also be aware of other forms of communication. A study conducted at UCLA in the late 1960s determined there are in fact three main ways in which we communicate with others. The three methods and the impact they have are as follows:

- Body language conveys 55% of our message
- Our voice conveys 38% of our message
- Our words convey 7% of our message

Most individuals are surprised to discover that words have the least impact on our audience and that our body movement and tone of voice have the greatest impact. People improperly use these two communication methods. As we are about to see, this hinders our opportunity to create positive images and reduces the effectiveness of our words.

At first you may find it hard to believe that body language and tone of voice are so important, but try this experiment: Drop your shoulders and head. Direct your eyes to the floor. Breathe slowly and in a shallow tempo. Take small slow steps and shuffle toward your spouse or another loved one. Speak slowly in a low monotone with no energy and excitement. Make sure your voice does not express sincerity. Now tell the person you love them with all your heart. Tell them how glad you are to be with them. You will notice that your spouse or loved one will look at you strangely and with disbelief. They will not feel the message you expressed with your words. They will only feel the message you expressed with your body movement and tone of your voice.

Now try this: When your spouse or loved one comes into view, run to them. Give them the biggest and widest smile you can make. Look directly into their eyes as you hug them. Allow your breathing to quicken, hug them tighter, and pull your body close to theirs. Now lay your face next to theirs for a few seconds. Next, kiss them softly on the cheeks and lips. Then softly whisper in their ear, "I don't love you." Then look them in the eyes and smile. Even though your words said you did not love them, your actions show you do. The person will feel the love you expressed with your body language and tone of voice. This is the message they will believe. They will react lovingly to your body language and tone of voice, and ignore your words.

To see how powerful body language and tone of voice are, imagine two speakers giving the same speech. One speaker shows excitement in his voice. He varies his tone by raising it when he wants to emphasize a point. His tone of voice is strong, warm and friendly. He uses powerful body gestures. He frequently smiles, laughs and develops eye contact with his audience. He moves powerfully, quickly and confidently as he addresses the audience. The audience listens intently to his every word and enjoys the entire message.

Another speaker delivers the same speech to a similar audience, but he speaks low, slowly and in a monotone. His body is tense and rigid. He does not smile or make eye contact. He makes no gestures. Needless to say, this person will bore his audience and they will hear little of his message.

Even though both speakers spoke identical words, they delivered entirely different messages to their audience. The first was effective. He established rapport with his audience because of the messages he projected through his body language and voice tone. The second speaker never established rapport because of the negative non-verbal messages he sent out.

As you can see, the words spoken in these imaginary speeches had the least impact on the audience. You've probably noticed the same phenomenon when two different people tell the same joke. One will have the audience laughing hysterically, while the other is booed off the stage.

It is important not to send mixed messages when you speak. Make sure your words are not sending one message while your body language and tone of voice are sending another. Do not misunderstand this important point: Your words are important, but the manner in which you use your body language and tone of voice to express them have the most impact.

To convey the proper message, your words, body language and tone of voice must be congruent. You must be aware when you are sending mixed signals. Your body language can project power and command respect; it can also project a lack of of these qualities. The following body language shows a lack of self respect:

• Playing with change	• Folded arms
• Fidgeting	• Hands clasped in front
• Tapping a pencil	• Scratching
• Slouched shoulders	• No eye contact
• Feet together	• Excessive movement
• Nail biting	• Hands in pocket

Do not project overbearing and negative body language. It is offensive and disrespectful to others and builds an atmosphere of uneasiness. It creates an invisible barrier between you and your audience. Examples of overbearing body language would be

• Glaring or staring eye contact	• Rigid posture
• Violating other people's space	• Hands on hips
• Tense facial expressions	• Offensive gestures
• Not allowing others to speak	• Pointing fingers

Show confidence, power and respect in your body language. Show you have a positive attitude about yourself and others. Your body language must show you work well with others. It must exhibit strength, warmth and intelligence.

We often send negative messages with our voices as well. We do this by speaking too loud, too fast or too slow. When we speak in questioning or unsure tones, or stammer, we show a lack of confidence. If our voice sounds threatening or offensive it turns listeners off. Stuttering can be an indication of nervousness and lack of self confidence. Making incoherent sounds ("um," "er," etc.) also suggests a lack of self control and confidence.

Always send positive messages with the tone of your voice and your body language. Make sure it's strong and confident. It must show genuine interest and enthusiasm when you speak. It must show you care about yourself and others.

Be Sensitive to Education Levels

Another element to building rapport is to match your listener's level of education, experience and expertise. The way we speak to college graduates or seasoned professionals is different from the way we speak to elementary schoolchildren. The message may be the same, but the way it's communicated is different. This is important if you have more education than the interviewer. Often long-term employees do not have the education younger employees do or are not current with new techniques or technology. Make them feel comfortable with you.

It's important to make interviewers aware of your education, training, skills, and expertise. It's even more important not to insult or ridicule interviewers because you have more education. If you are interviewing with someone who has less education, be considerate of their feelings. When you discuss education, suggest how fortunate you were to have the opportunity to go to school. Never put down individuals who have less education. Say how important it is to combine education with experience. Let them know experience is just as important as education. Tell them you look forward to learning from their valuable experience. Show that combining your education with their experience makes a winning team. This is an important message to convey during interviews. Interviewers with limited education often fear hiring employees who may replace them. Show interviewers how they will benefit from your knowledge. It will make them feel comfortable and secure.

Make sure you don't offend interviewers. Do not give advice unless they ask you for it. Telling interviewers how to run their departments during interviews is one way *not* to get hired. Stress you are a team player and are not looking to take the interviewer's position. This should be done in a subtle manner. An exception to this rule is when interviewers are looking for applicants to replace current employees. In this case, indicate you look forward to being promoted when a position becomes available.

Appearance

God looks to the heart but human nature makes mortals look at our appearance. Looking your best helps you achieve success (it does not *make* you a success, however). This starts with being clean and well groomed. Make sure your hands and nails are clean. Keep your hair properly cut and combed. If you wear cologne or perfume, it must not be excessive or offensive.

Dress for success. Make sure you dress properly and look your best. Your manner of dress must be similar to that of employees who work in the position you are applying for. This does not mean you have to have expensive clothes or wear the latest styles. It means making the most of what you have. Your clothes must be clean, properly pressed, and odor-free.

If you are 20 pounds or more overweight, it's in your best interest to lose unhealthy and unsightly pounds and inches. Being overweight is detrimental to your health. It will rob you of energy and stamina that you need to be competitive. Being grossly overweight is an indication you are not in control of your life and have a lack of respect for yourself. If you are overweight, don't focus on your weight during interviews. The time to focus on losing weight is before interviews. Make the best of your current situation. Wear loose-fitting clothes that complement you. If your clothes are too tight alter them. Be neat, clean and comfortable in your clothes.

* * *

Interviewing is not the most enjoyable activity. We often become frustrated because of the large number of unsuccessful interviews we undergo. We start to see ourselves as failures. We must not allow these frustrations to overcome us and adversely affect our lives.

One effective method to overcome these frustrations is to establish new rules for ourselves that prevent us from failing. We must approach each interview with a primary and secondary goal. The primary goal is to obtain the position. If we are unsuccessful in an interview, we can fall back on our secondary goal. Our secondary goal should be to learn as much possible to ensure success in our next interview. Review interviews objectively and honestly. Identify mistakes and weaknesses. Take immediate steps to correct them. Whenever we use failure to improve ourselves, we cannot fail. The more "no's" we experience the closer we are to a "yes."

One of the best ways to overcome feeling sorry for yourself is to help others who are less fortunate. Perform volunteer work in your free time. You will learn new skills and help others at the same time. Volunteer work is an excellent vehicle for making important contacts and gaining valuable experience. Include volunteer work on your resumé and use it as a selling point during your interviews.

Between interviews make the most of your free time. Use it to update or develop new skills that will make you competitive. There are many excellent self-help programs out there. Toastmasters and other organizations focus on improving members' public speaking and presentation skills through courses, books and videotapes. Colleges offer courses and seminars for assertiveness training, public speaking, and developing leadership skills. Acting and dance classes can help bring you out of your shell. Arts and crafts work-shops can develop your creativity. The possibilities are endless. Your new professional and personal skills will make you appealing to prospective employers.

Now is the time to take stock of yourself and review your options. Many people have discovered that *not* being hired was the best thing that ever happened to them. It was a blessing in disguise. It forced them to take actions they would never have taken if they were employed. Many successful businesses were started by individuals who were unable to find employment with other companies.

You are in control of your life when you make things happen instead of waiting for something to happen. Successful people have one thing in common: They know how to make things happen for themselves and others.

Chapter 6

Establish a New Career

All that a man achieves and all that he fails to achieve is the direct result of his own thoughts
—James Allen

IF YOU'VE FOLLOWED the advice given in the previous chapters, you will eventually land the position you've always wanted. Take the time to celebrate attaining this milestone. You've reached an important goal in your career plan. Now the real fun begins.

Getting the position you desire is another step toward success, but it doesn't mean you can now sit back and coast. At one time, you would be given a chance to settle in to your new position. In the New Economy, if you can't show your value to an employer within a few months of being hired, you may find yourself back on the job hunt. Markets and technology change so quickly today that employers cannot afford to keep employees who do not fit in or do not show their value to the company. The impression you make in the first few months in a new position will determine your success with your employer.

As I've explained earlier, having useful skills and working hard do not guarantee success. This remains true in the early days of a new job. You were hired for your skills and your willingness to work hard. Now you have to prove that you will be an asset to the company. You have to continue to sell yourself as you did during your interview. We are the product of our thoughts. We must start with a strong belief we will succeed regardless of prior experiences. It does not matter what other people believe. What matters is that we believe in ourselves and will work to achieve our goals.

We demonstrate strong beliefs by taking proper actions. When we do, we convert non-believers into believers in our goals. They see a person with a mission whom they can respect. No matter what position or career you have, always perform at your best. It does not matter if others are smarter, stronger or have more resources. There will always be others who have more talent, experience or knowledge. Believing in yourself is the key to success.

Wisdom and Knowledge

Another element essential for a successful career is the ability to make the most of available resources. Wisdom is the key to accomplishing this task. There is a difference between knowledge and wisdom. Wisdom is the ability to use knowledge effectively. We waste knowledge when we fail to put it to use. Many highly educated individuals fail in their careers because they lack wisdom. It is wisdom that sustains victory and the successes in our lives. It allows us to adapt and grow in a changing environment. Wisdom allows us to make the most of situations and use our skills and talents to the best of our abilities.

Wise people never worry about what they don't have. They are more concerned about maximizing what they do have. Wisdom requires thinking before we act or speak. Individuals with wisdom develop different mindsets. Wisdom allows them to see things objectively. They identify their needs and then make sound plans to obtain what they need. Wisdom is our most powerful tool.

Adversity

Prepare for adversity. It is a daily part of our lives. Successful people make adversity work for them. Once you develop this attitude you will create and sustain a successful career. People who are born rich will not stay rich if they don't learn to handle adversity.

We cannot be successful if we can't overcome the adversities we inevitably encounter in our careers and lives. People with successful careers encounter greater adversities than people with less successful careers. The higher the position, the greater the responsibilities and adversities. Never run from or ignore adversity. If you do, your problems will become more severe and will haunt you for life.

Enjoy the Process

Enjoy the process of working. Don't wait for happiness to happen until after you achieve your goals. Goals can take a lifetime to complete. This is too long to endure without receiving satisfaction from your work. The reason why we fail to complete goals is that we find little satisfaction during the process of trying to achieve them. It is essential to enjoy the process of achieving our goals. It helps us complete long-term goals and overcome difficulties. Reward yourself for doing good work. Don't reward yourself for merely *planning* to do it. If you promise yourself something for completing an assignment, make sure you keep it. When we make false promises to ourselves, our subconscious stops believing us. It then rebels against us. You never want to create this internal conflict.

Successful careers do not happen by accident; they are created by design. Let's look at some strategies for creating success.

Know What You Want

In chapter 1 we discussed the importance of advance preparation for your career. Know what you want. Do not base decisions and actions on what others want from you. Take the time to know yourself. Learn what you want and what makes you happy. Be willing to experiment and explore different situations. Use them to discover your talents and what you enjoy.

You cannot give happiness to others when you are unhappy. Doing work you do not love or enjoy is often life's greatest frustration. Follow the steps outlined in chapter 1 — they are essential.

Once they are completed, you will move in the right direction. Even after you follow the steps outlined in chapter 1 you will need to make changes once you start your career. This is called personal growth and maturity.

When we first start our careers, we are inexperienced, naive, and lack critical knowledge. To overcome these problems, learn how to be successful. Ask successful employees how they became successful in their careers. Seek their advice and experience. Model yourself after successful people. Find what qualities and skills they possess. Learn how they acquired those skills and qualities.

Make friends with successful people and learn as much as possible from them. Don't just look for what they can do for you, but find out how you can help them. Strong relationships are developed and maintained by a willingness to give and to receive. When possible, find mentors. Successful people enjoy being mentors.

Work Intelligently

What I am about to say goes against the grain of what we are taught all our lives, so it is difficult for people to understand: *Working hard does not guarantee or ensure success.* If you believe hard work alone will ensure your success, you are greatly mistaken. In fact, this belief will ensure you fail not only in your career but in life as well. Many hard-working people never establish a viable, rewarding career. They often find little happiness and live a meager existence.

If we are not able to use our labor to enhance our lives and those of others, we are working ineffectively. Working smart and with a predefined purpose is the key to success. It's far more effective than just working hard.

Nothing is wrong with hard work when it produces the results you desire. When hard work does not produce the desired results, something is wrong. The problem may be you, the way you are doing it, or a combination of both. Working smart is the ability to produce the best possible results with the least amount of effort and time. Working smart is not looking for shortcuts that result in inadequate work. Working smart requires planning and preparation. It requires commitment to performing the best possible work and seeking ways to improve performance.

To work intelligently we must master the art of listening. Effective listening places us ahead of our competition. Many of us tune out the world around us. We intentionally become deaf when important information is given. We do not listen because we feel the information is a waste of time, or we don't want to hear what is being said. Often we do not listen effectively, due to our inability to concentrate. These are mistakes that can be fatal to careers. We miss out on valuable opportunities because we did not hear what was said. We are unaware of people's needs, therefore we cannot help others.

Most people only take the time to listen to important people. This is disastrous. Everybody has important information. Their information can be the difference between success and failure. Fortunes have been lost because people overlooked valuable information (i.e., they did not listen).

Never expect something for nothing. Success does not come overnight. The sooner we realize there are no shortcuts to success, the sooner we create success. Working intelligently requires paying our dues. Paying our dues means we must be willing to start at the bottom and work to the top. Paying dues means we are willing to do the best work possible. We do this even if we dislike our work and salary.

Successful people take pride in their work. They have the ability to turn problems into opportunities that allow them to grow. They use what they learn to achieve their final goals. Few career paths are straight lines. Be willing to work past obstacles to reach your final destination. Learn from your mistakes. Show you are flexible, trustworthy and dependable.

When we pay our dues we earn respect from our peers and superiors. Respect is a quality that is earned and not given freely or automatically. Respect creates opportunities that open doors. If you are in a new position, paying your dues is the only legitimate way to earn respect. It is more important for others to respect you as a person than just the position or title you hold.

Show respect to others even if they do not show respect to you. Respecting others shows you are disciplined and respect yourself. Just because you respect others does not mean they will respect you. Never take it personally. When individuals do not respect themselves, they are incapable of respecting others. Their lack of self esteem is *their* problem, not yours.

Maintain focus, know what is important. Stay on top of priorities. Everyday we are bombarded with distractions. They range from minor to major problems (phone calls, visitors, emergencies, etc.). This does not mean you should ignore distractions. It means you must handle distractions without losing your focus. Allowing distractions to consume your thoughts and time will cause you to fail. Distractions are a daily part of our lives. Develop effective ways to control and handle them. Never allow distractions to disrupt or control your life.

Create Worthwhile Goals

Establishing worthwhile goals is impossible if you have no idea of your direction. Desires, interests, and beliefs drive goals. If you never discover them, establishing worthwhile goals is impossible. Striving to be the best and staying on top is easier when we have a career we love. We invest valuable time learning to play games, gossiping, and so on, but we are often unwilling to devote the time needed to discover our true selves. This is a great tragedy.

When starting new careers, plan short- and long-term goals. Learn as much as you can about your employer and your career. Learn all company positions. Obtain organizational charts and company directories, and talk with employees. Find out what positions exist, even if they are not vacant.

After you have completed your review, determine what position you desire as your final goal. If the position is a high-level one, list each position you must obtain to achieve your final one. Next, establish realistic time frames for obtaining each position. This is critical. Time frames are guides to determine if what you are doing is working. This allows you to monitor progress and make adjustments if you are off track.

Write your ultimate goal on a three-by-five card so you can review it daily. Make a list of the skills, education and training that are vital to your success. Indicate the ones you possess and the ones you must obtain.

Next, develop a written plan to obtain needed skills, education and training. Make sure plans are written in detail. They must include completion dates to monitor your progress. List important company players who can give you training and experience. Find out what type of people they hire. Work with them whenever possible.

If you don't have opportunities to work with people who can influence your career, create opportunities to do so. After you or others make recommendations, ask to work on these projects. Get involved in company task forces and steering committees. Network within and outside the company. Find powerful mentors to help you succeed. Do extra work without being asked or expecting financial rewards. Show you not only enjoy learning but enjoy sharing your talents, experience, and skills with others. Show management and co-workers you are a team player.

The Ability to Adapt

If you are not getting the results you desire, then you need to make changes. It may not mean working harder, but it does mean working smarter. You may need to change your attitude, learn new skills or obtain more education, or develop more productive ways to work. Fools are individuals who are not satisfied with their results but continue to do the identical thing over and over again and expect different results. Don't be a fool; if what you are doing is not working, don't continue to do it.

This does not mean throw in the towel and give up. It means make an assessment of what you are doing and determine why it is not working. Once you identify the problem you can develop solutions.

If your goal is to get to the opposite side of a three-foot-thick steel wall, review your options. Your first thought may be to break through the wall. This can be impossible if you do not have the proper tools and equipment. You can spend the rest of your life beating on the wall with a stick and your fist and never succeed. If you are willing to review your options, you may be able to easily get to the other side. With the stick and your hands you can dig a hole under the wall and crawl to the other side, or you could climb over the wall. You may also find out that if you walk south for a mile the wall ends and you can walk around it.

As you can see from this little parable, there are usually a number of ways to accomplish the same goal. Often the first methods we come up with are not feasible. If we continued to try to break through the wall we would have never gotten to the other side. By reviewing our options and trying new approaches, we can turn failure into success. Always review your options. It's a key to success.

Visionaries

The difference between a successful and a mediocre career is the ability to see the world in a different light. Successful individuals see problems as opportunities to improve situations. They do not approach management for answers to their problems. Instead, they approach management with *solutions* to their problems.

From the start of your career make it a habit to never approach your boss with a problem without a solution, preferably more than one. Your solution may or may not be correct, but it shows initiative, leadership qualities, and problem-solving abilities. It shows you can handle responsibilities. Managers are not fond of employees who always run to them with problems or complaints without solutions. They consider them major headaches. Managers love employees who develop solutions to problems. They want them on their team and find them invaluable and unique. They feel comfortable with them. Management will give such employees additional responsibilities and opportunities such as promotions and high-visibility assignments.

Individuals with successful careers are visionaries. They see things before they exist and before others think of them. They don't wait for problems to arise before changing situations and conditions to improve the quality of work, increase efficiency, and reduce costs. They are the individuals who develop new technology or are the first to use it. These individuals can take risks as described in chapter 1. Instead of waiting for things to happen, they *make* things happen. They stand above the crowd and contribute to their employer's success.

Chapter 7

Reinvent Your Career

He who has goods can sell them.

—NIGERIAN PROVERB

*Our nettlesome task is to discover how to organize our
strength into compelling power.*

—MARTIN LUTHER KING, JR.

OFTEN we reach an impasse in our careers. We are no longer excited about what we do. We no longer see our careers as enjoyable. We only see them as a way to make money. In other cases, we feel overworked, underpaid and treated unfairly. We feel cheated and resent our employers, superiors and co-workers. With this type of attitude it is impossible to stay focused or perform properly.

Often it's not what's going on in our careers, but what's going on in our lives that's the problem. We allow situations in our lives to cloud our judgment. We make improper rationalizations. We blame our frustrations on the actions of others. When we reach this point, we are in big trouble. It shows a lack of control in our careers and lives. It is critical that we regain control of our careers and lives by changing our thinking and redefining our goals.

It starts with an honest assessment of ourselves. We are often our own worst enemy. We unintentionally or intentionally turn on a self-destruct switch. We use negative thoughts and actions as fuel to sabotage our careers and success. Instead of cultivating our careers, we stifle them. We allow weeds (i.e., our negative thoughts) to grow and strangle our careers. When we neglect our careers they become barren and die. This starts when we focus all our time and energy on external situations and ignore internal problems. Internal problems are problems within ourselves.

The first step in revamping our careers is to do an in-depth self examination. We must determine what is troubling us and how it is affecting our careers. Often we have allowed one or more incidents to bruise our egos, which has left us with a perpetually negative attitude. We allow this negative attitude to adversely affect our thinking and our work. Instead of spending time on important matters, we waste it on non-productive activities (anger, revenge, jealousy, etc.).

Rather than automatically blame others for our failure to receive promotions, recognition or satisfaction in our careers, we should first examine ourselves. We must ask ourselves, Was I the best person for that position? Did I properly apply myself in my career? Do I have the skills, training, abilities, education, and desire to properly perform the work? Unsuccessful or dissatisfying careers are due not to the faults of others but to our own shortcomings. We neglect to do the things mandatory for successful careers.

It's natural and easy to blame others for our failures. Successful and satisfying careers require a great deal of time, planning, and effort. Most individuals are not willing to put forth the time, effort and energy to create a rewarding career. Instead of taking responsibility for their failures they prefer to blame others. This is a common ploy of individuals with unsuccessful careers. Blaming others is a way of eliminating their responsibility.

These techniques may remove guilt and responsibility but they will also rob you of power and control over your career. This unfair exchange will make you a loser. As previously indicated, successful individuals effectively deal with obstacles and adversity. They don't blame others or situations for what they do or don't do. They do not allow others to control their careers or lives. Instead, they accept full responsibility for their successes and failures. They view failures as valuable experiences.

If you are not satisfied with your career and want to revamp it, you must accept that *you and you alone are responsible for the success or failure of your career.* This means you are willing to work to overcome obstacles by taking charge and accepting responsibility. Once you accept responsibility for your success or failure, you will gain control over your life.

Your next step is to make an honest assessment of yourself. Identify strengths and weaknesses. Establish a mission for yourself, then create worthwhile goals to support your mission. The goals must include developing and mastering the skills you need to be successful in your career. They must include time frames to determine if you are on track or if you need to make changes.

Take control of your career. Be willing to make tough decisions and adhere to them. It may be necessary to seek employment elsewhere or make career changes. Before making drastic changes, be sure you are making them for the right reasons. Individuals often quit or run away from problems rather than deal with them. If you handle your problems in this manner, you will never find success.

On the other hand, you may work under conditions where it is not in your best interest to stay. When your career has become obsolete or your environment limits opportunities or is detrimental, it is time to move on. Know the difference between running from problems and making smart career moves that will empower you.

Creating Success Day-to-Day

Most of us neglect to follow fundamentals essential to success. We show poor judgment and fail to use common sense. We overlook the importance of treating people fairly and respectfully. We disregard the significance of good attendance and punctuality. Even if we produce excellent work, deficiencies in these areas can lead to our downfall.

After many of us achieve success, we tend to overlook the qualities that made us successful. We must continue to do the things that made us successful if we want to continue our success. The qualities that propelled us to success are the same qualities that keep us successful.

Solving the cumulative, small, day-to-day problems is vital to success. Many of us fail because we allow our emotions to control us.

When we make subjective decisions based on emotions and not on facts, it is disastrous. Use common sense. Without common sense our judgment easily becomes clouded. Common sense allows us to think objectively and make responsible decisions.

Using common sense does not mean acting and thinking the same as others. In fact, most successful people think and act differently from the majority but demonstrate common sense. Successful people see things before they exist and are willing to work to achieve what they desire. They use common sense to achieve their goals in the most productive manner.

Show Courtesy and Respect

Showing courtesy and respect is the best way to win respect and support. When we are courteous and respectful to others, it shows we respect ourselves and others. People enjoy working with or for individuals who show courtesy and respect for them.

You will not have to look for good employees when you treat people well. Good employees will wait in line for you. They do not do this just for the position but for the chance to work with you. Treating people with courtesy and respect creates a positive working environment conducive to superior work. It eliminates unnecessary stress and tension.

People with low self-esteem falsely believe if you show kindness it is a sign of weakness and people will take advantage of you. They incorrectly believe people only respect you if they fear you. When we treat people unkindly, they will plot our downfall at every turn. If they are not actively involved in plotting our downfall, they support others who are.

Treating people with courtesy and respect doesn't mean we cannot be demanding. Some of the most demanding people are courteous and respectful. Their confidence allows them to treat others the way they want to be treated. They know people perform better when treated with respect.

When employees are unable to produce, respectful managers take appropriate action. This means properly evaluating the situation.

Their decision may require counseling, retraining, transfer to a better-suited position, or termination. During this process they treat employees with respect. They also make them aware of what is expected and what the outcome will be if these expectations are not met. They never intentionally degrade employees whose work performance is not up to par. They never base their decisions and actions on malice, anger or revenge. They base them on work performance and other important factors. They do not receive pleasure from disciplining or firing employees. When possible they try to help these employees.

People who are unable to show courtesy and respect for others usually have personal problems. It often is a sign of insecurity and frustration. Because of their unhappiness, they want others to feel bad. These problems also arise when people are not properly trained to supervise. Both situations are indications there are problems. It is worthwhile to take ongoing "people skills" courses (e.g., how to communicate with others, how to manage people effectively or deal with negative situations). These courses provide guidance and the confidence to overcome managerial deficiencies.

Attendance and Punctuality

Just because you work hard, don't get into the habit of coming to work late. Never allow yourself to become comfortable with the excuse, "I worked late last night so I can come in late or when I want to." If you have a problem getting up in the morning, change your starting hours to a later time. Instead of starting at 8:00 a.m. start at 9:00 a.m. Many companies provide flexible hours.

People notice when you come in late but do not notice when you work late hours. Often they are not working when you work late. When employees see other employees and supervisors come in late it makes them resentful and causes them to lose respect for the offenders. When employees see supervisors arriving late, they may feel it is okay to do the same. This starts a chain reaction leading to a loss of productivity.

Just as important as punctuality is attendance. We can easily find an excuse not to come to work. We seldom feel 100%. Don't allow yourself to look for reasons to skip work. Inept employees use sick time when they don't feel like doing a project or when the going gets tough. These individuals quickly develop a reputation for being unsuitable for more responsibility or advancement.

These same employees use their allotted sick leave each year. Unsuccessful employees tell themselves, "If I don't use my sick time I will lose it." Ask yourself what is more important — losing sick days, or losing opportunities for advancement, higher salaries and personal satisfaction. If you're not around you miss out on opportunities and reduce your chances for success.

Of course, there is nothing wrong with using sick time when you are legitimately ill. Your boss won't be happy if you give everyone else in the office the flu. Also, if you don't give your body a chance to fully recover, you'll find yourself getting sick again soon.

Studies show there is a direct correlation between good attendance and punctuality and success. Individuals who have good attendance records and are punctual are more likely to be successful. They show enthusiasm and set a good example for fellow employees.

* * *

In this chapter we've looked at reasons why careers stall. If you have trouble seeing why you have not progressed, get feedback from others — family, friends, and co-workers. Don't get angry if you hear something you don't like — after all, you've asked for it — but consider their comments and advice objectively. Remember, the goal of this assessment is to reinvent your career and get back on the track to success.

As I've said before, the best time to assess your career is before the situation becomes dire. Being successful requires constant reassessment of ourselves and our goals. Everyone has ups and downs in their careers. Expect it to happen to you and do what you can to prepare for it.

Chapter 8

Creating Permanent Security

He who starts behind in the great race of life must forever remain behind or run faster than the man in front.
—BENJAMIN E. MAYS

Education is our passport to the future, for tomorrow belongs to the people who prepare for it today.
—MALCOLM X

THE lack of security in their careers is a major concern of North Americans. This dilemma is greater for African Americans. Their rate of unemployment is often more than double that of white Americans. Black workers have greater concerns about security with their employers. An article published by the *Wall Street Journal,* "Losing Ground, in The Latest Recession, Only Blacks Suffered Net Employment Loss" (September 14, 1993), verified this. Using employment data supplied by employers to the Equal Employment Opportunity Commission (EEOC), the authors reviewed the job losses of whites, blacks, Hispanics, and Asians for 1990–91. The study showed that blacks were up to 3.56 times more likely to lose their jobs than other races.

This is an alarming statistic for new and long-term black employees. Today companies are closing plants and going out of business in record numbers. Profits are down or nonexistent in many formerly profitable companies. Many positions have been eliminated. African Americans are feeling the greatest impact of job losses.

Unemployed blacks, other minorities, and women are fearful that they will never find successful careers. They believe they will be forced to accept non-rewarding and low-paying positions.

Companies and employees not only face competition from other American employees and companies, but from foreign markets as well. Foreign competitors are allowed to pay workers less then minimum wages and do not provide costly benefits. Foreign companies do not adhere to strict government regulation. Some foreign governments subsidize their companies, and provide them with tax breaks and low-interest government loans.

To be competitive and to meet these challenges American companies and their employees must work together to be more efficient and reduce costs. Companies are reducing the number of top and middle-management and low-level employees. In the past only unskilled laborers lacked job security. Today, for the first time in our history, there are equal numbers of skilled and unskilled unemployed. Employees are in a state of panic and confusion. We no longer have our security blankets. The American dream has become the American nightmare.

Our dilemma is that the employment market has changed dramatically over the last 10 years and our work force has failed to change with it. Twenty-five years ago it was considered normal to have one career and work for one employer for life. Fifteen years ago it was considered normal to change employers or positions every six years. Today it is considered normal to change employment every three or four years.

At one time, if you worked hard, were loyal and had seniority, you were guaranteed security. These career rules no longer apply. In fact, long-term employees are often the first targeted for laid off, due to the cost of their benefits (vacations, profit sharing, pensions, medical coverage, etc.) and higher salaries.

Any employees who look to companies for security are setting themselves up for disappointment. It's like the song, "Looking for Love in All the Wrong Places," but instead, it's employees looking for *security* in all the wrong places. Companies no longer provide long- or short-term security.

This leads us to the question, How and where do we find security in our careers today? The first step is to change old rules that no longer apply. We must create new rules that work in today's competitive environment. We can no longer look for security in the companies we work for or the careers we chose. We need to stop "looking for security in all the wrong places." Career security is created within ourselves and is determined by proper planning and actions. The following determine our career security:

- Our level of current skills and abilities
- Our ability to market our skills
- Our ability to recognize demand for our services
- Our ability to create a demand for our services
- Our ability to be self sufficient
- Our ability to recognize opportunities
- Our ability to transfer our skills and abilities

Our current skills and talents are what make us valuable to employers or customers. If there is not a demand for our skills we must possess the ability to create demand for them. Our skills must be transferable to other employers or industries.

Having marketable, transferable skills is important, but is not in itself sufficient to make our careers secure. We must also recognize and use opportunities to ensure our success. We must possess the abilities to reach sufficient markets to sell our skills to employers. The best products or services in the world will not sell if no one knows about them. We must be self sufficient and not depend on others for our careers and income.

If your skills and abilities are limited, so are your compensation, security and opportunities. This will continue regardless of how hard you work. Hard work alone is not enough. Employers can always find employees who work hard. The same employers can never find enough employees who make substantial contributions to the success of their companies. These employees' skills, abilities, and talents can turn a failing company into a prosperous one.

Too many employees spend too much time and energy working hard and not enough on developing their skills. They fail to make proper investments in themselves. As a result, their contributions eventually become limited and too costly. The likelihood grows that they will lose their jobs. Most long-term employees do not have sufficient skills to find a comparable position outside their current employer. They do not possess marketable skills to compete. New and younger employees are able to provide better service in less time, at reduced cost, and with less effort. They are trained to use modern technology which enhances their work performance. When we keep our skills current we improve our value to employers. If you lack sufficient skills, you must change this situation.

To create career security, make yourself invaluable to employers. Be the best possible employee you can be. Don't do it for your employer; do it for yourself. Place yourself in a position where your employer would suffer the greatest loss if your employment is terminated. Develop transferable skills and talents that will make others seek your services. Create a winning relationship for you and your employer. Make it a goal to improve yourself and your working environment.

If you get nothing else out of this book but the next statement, you can create a life where you will never be unemployed or unable to earn a satisfying income: *In America today there are more opportunities to establish rewarding careers and earn more money than ever dreamed possible.* With today's technology and information resources, a creative mind and a willingness to take action, we all can create rewarding and secure careers for ourselves. Valuable opportunities are presented each day but you must take advantage of them.

It would be untruthful to say creating permanent and lucrative careers is easy. However, regardless of the difficulty, it is possible for everyone. It is easier than being unemployed and living in fear without an income. The key to success is a change in our attitudes. If you can't find employment, create employment. For instance, many blacks are upset that foreigners are opening businesses in their communities. Many of these newcomers have no formal education and speak little English. Yet against all these obstacles, they succeed. They establish independence and security. The reason for their success is quite simple: They know what they want and are willing to work and save for it. They will not accept failure.

You may ask how people create such determination. The answer is simple. Their culture teaches them they must depend on themselves for survival. They learn from childhood to provide for themselves or die. The societies they came from did not provide welfare, unemployment, disability benefits, workers' compensation or social security. They had to adapt to their environment and take advantage of every opportunity.

These people know that making excuses for failure or being paralyzed by fear will not provide food, clothing or shelter. They do not allow poor English to prevent them from owning a business. They learn the skills they need to operate their business. They learn how to count and where to buy discount merchandise. They are willing to work for others to learn these things. They have no problem with starting at the bottom. They make sacrifices daily to achieve their long-term goals. They are willing to work and help their own people. Instead of resenting others for their success, they emulate them.

Learn from these people and use this knowledge to create your own success story. Duplicate what successful people do. These valuable lessons are free. Learn by observing others.

Permanent security arises through a process of evolution. Being on top and having a secure career today does not guarantee career security tomorrow. Permanent career security requires adapting to constant change, being a keen observer, learning and re-learning, and looking to the future. Being the biggest, strongest or the smartest does not create career security.

To illustrate this point, look to the past. What happened to the dinosaurs? More then 165 million years ago, hundreds of different species of dinosaurs roamed the earth. The brontosaurus was one of the largest dinosaurs. It was approximately 70 feet long and 40 feet high. It weighted more then 32 metric tons. It was one of the largest and strongest creatures that ever walked the face of the earth. Yet the brontosaur became extinct along with all the other dinosaurs. The most widely accepted theory for why dinosaurs became extinct is they were unable to adapt to their changing environment.

No matter how big and important and secure our careers may seem, they too will become extinct if we do not adapt to our changing environment. In fact, just adapting to change is not enough. We must prepare for changes *before* they happen. Only with proper planning can we adjust to changes in an efficient and timely fashion. Avoid career extinction by creating a new one. Create permanent security in your career by preparing for changes before they occur.

It is each individual's duty, not only to themselves but to their families, to accept the responsibility of creating permanent career security. If you are not willing to do this you are negligent, irresponsible, and lazy. You cannot rely on your existing career, employer, friends, family or God to do this for you. God helps those who help themselves. God does this when you believe in Him and obey his words. "Laziness brings on deep sleep, and the shiftless man goes hungry" (Proverbs 19:15).

Skills, talent, ideas, experience and energy create security. We must have something to offer employers. If you don't have sufficient skills, now is the time to obtain them. Learn how to provide for yourself. Remember the early pioneers. They were self-sufficient. In our civilized society most of us have lost the ability to be self-sufficient. Being employed gives us a false sense of security.

Always be on the look-out for ways to become more self-sufficient. Constantly re-evaluate your present thinking. A company does not owe you employment because you work for them. A company owes you fair pay, fair treatment, and equal opportunity during employment. The only one who owes you anything is you. You have a responsibility to learn as much as you can and to keep your skills current.

We often fail to establish permanent security for ourselves because we fail to overcome our fears. We allow our fears to prevent us from achieving our dreams. Our fears prevent us from taking advantage of opportunities. Our fear of failure prevents us from growing and learning. Our fears create a form of paralysis that stifles our careers. Having a job gives us a false sense of security. A job or career in itself does not provide security; our present skills, abilities, and marketing expertise do.

Depend on yourself and not a company, job or career. Consider yourself as a business that must sell the best product to secure its future.Control your fears by facing them. There is nothing wrong with fear when it is used properly. It prevents us from harming ourselves and endangering others. Fear becomes our enemy and counterproductive when it restricts and reduces the quality of our lives. Never allow foolish fear to prevent you from making the right decisions and creating permanent security. Franklin Roosevelt explained it this way: "Let me assert my firm belief that the only thing we have to fear is fear itself — nameless, unreasoning, unjustified terror which paralyzes needed efforts to convert retreat into advance."

Create reasonable expectations for yourself. Start by learning to depend on yourself rather than others. A friend of mine was fortunate. His parents were financially well off. They bought him everything when he was a child. They even paid his way through college, bought him a new car and paid the rent for his apartment while he was in school. In his freshman year he was a straight A student.

My parents could not afford to pay for my education. I had to work full- and part-time jobs to support myself during college. In my freshman year I was not a straight A student. In fact, I failed my Accounting 101 class. My friend teased me so much about it that we made a bet. I was initially a Business Administration major but I changed my major to Accounting. I did this because my friend majored in accounting. We bet that whoever graduated with the lower grade point average would pay the other a hundred dollars.

I graduated with a degree in accounting and with a higher GPA. Before we graduated my friend changed his major from Accounting to Business Administration. The classes became too difficult for him. You see, he was used to people helping him or taking over when things became difficult.

This situation continued when he was employed in his first professional position. He worked for a prestigious insurance company in a managerial training program. In the late seventies he was the only black in an executive management training program. White employees were not used to working with or taking orders from a black supervisor. My friend became so uncomfortable with the situation he asked to speak with the president. He informed the president that if the white employees did not treat him better he would resign. The president informed him it would take time to change white employees' attitudes to accept him.

My friend told the president this was not good enough and he was resigning. The president immediately called his secretary and told her to prepare my friend's final paycheck. My friend was shocked. He never imagined the president would accept his offer to resign. He believed he was invaluable and would have his way. This incident destroyed my friend's confidence and self-esteem. He was not prepared to deal with the option he had proposed.

Whenever you make important decisions, never play a hand you cannot afford to lose. My friend was unable to keep a position after this experience. He developed emotional problems and became unstable. He ended up living on the streets. Through this sad story, I discovered I was the truly fortunate one. My circumstances growing up, though hard, had given me resilience and the strength to overcome adversity. My friend never learned to handle difficult situations growing up. He was not prepared to handle such situations as an adult. His sheltered upbringing had led him to establish unreasonable expectations for himself and others.

This does not mean we should accept less than what we want. It means we must strive to obtain our goals and desires with all our might. We must also learn to go on with our lives when things don't go our way. To be successful we must learn when and how to make compromises. We have not failed if we make compromises that ensure our success. Compromise allows us flexibility and provides us unlimited choices and opportunities.

We must be careful how and why we make compromises, however. We should only compromise when it adds value and power to our lives. We should not make compromises that go against our morals and principles. We should not make unethical compromises as an easy way out of a difficult situation.

Develop the skills and conviction to make the correct compromises. One way to determine when not to compromise is to ask yourself these questions: Will I lose respect for myself if I make this compromise? Is this decision morally wrong, unethical or against my principles? Will this be a bad decision over time? If your answers are yes, do not compromise your values. Your decision may cause short-term difficulties, but in the end, you will find you made the right choice.

Creating a Successful Career

You will find success quickly if you show others how to become successful. When you provide opportunities for others to share in your success, they will not only seek you out but support you as well. When you find individuals who support your goals you will find the road to success easier, enjoyable and obtainable.

Learning to persuade others to support you is one of the largest hurdles standing in the way of your success. Learn the art of persuasion. Convincing people it is to their advantage to help you is the most effective way to win them over. When people believe it is in their best interest to help you, you will find more help than you'll ever need.

Develop an Attitude of Gratitude

Appreciate not just the major things in life but the simple things as well. Make the most of every experience. An African-American professional who worked in a corporate environment for 20 years told me it had been a waste of his time. He said he never learned anything worthwhile during his career. This individual changed jobs every year and always complained he was never promoted. Whenever he referred to his former jobs or supervisors, it was always in negative terms. He blamed others for every bad thing that happened in his career.

It is impossible to succeed with such a negative attitude and closed mind. You create more work for yourself by not learning from each experience. You will make the same mistakes repeatedly. Never allow yourself to develop a negative frame of mind. This, along with an unwillingness to learn, is the foundation for failure.

Sell Yourself

Talent and abilities are not sufficient to guarantee success in your career. Learn to sell yourself and your abilities to others. When you learn how to sell yourself and your ideas, nothing is impossible to accomplish. Learning to sell your ideas makes it possible for dreams to come true. When you sell others on your ideas, they will support your goals as if they were their own.

To give you an idea of how important it is to sell yourself and your ideas, think of the story of Lee Iacocca. He saved Chrysler Corporation from extinction. In his book, *Iacocca: An Autobiography*, he explains how he sold his ideas to the unions, congress, creditors, banks, management, line employees and the public. He needed all parties to agree to his plans before he could turn Chrysler into a profitable business.

You must believe in your ideas before you can sell them to others and persuade them to join you. Before you ask others to do what seems impossible, you must believe you can do the impossible. Believing in your ideas is the only way you appear believable to others. Only when you show confidence in your abilities will you sell others on your ideas.

You may feel you will never be in a situation where you will need to sell your ideas to others. This couldn't be further from the truth. To be successful in any career or profession you must possess the ability to sell yourself. Let's test this theory. Suppose you are a janitor and are having difficulties performing your job because your equipment and supplies are inadequate. Your brooms and mops are old and worn. Your mop pail is too small and leaks water. You have to make unnecessary trips to refill your pail with water to mop the floor. You spend a great deal of time going back and forth to the basement to refill your mop pail. The detergent is not a quality product and does not properly clean the floor. You must mop the floor repeatedly to clean it.

New brooms, mops, pails and better-quality detergents are needed to perform your work properly. You know your boss does not want to spend additional money on these things. To accomplish this task you must sell your ideas to your boss. You can accomplish this by showing it's in your company's best interest to perform your work properly and efficiently. You must show that with the proper equipment you can clean the floors faster and more thoroughly. In fact, you can clean more rooms and floors better and in a shorter period. This could result in using fewer employees or allowing you to do additional work during your shift. These benefits would far exceed the small cost of additional equipment and supplies, will reduce costs over time, and increase profits.

When you use this approach to sell ideas, you change "no's" into "yes's." You will obtain the equipment, tools, supplies and support you need to be successful in your career. As you can now see, it does not matter if you have the highest-level management position or the lowest-level position. Work becomes easier when you master the art of selling yourself and your ideas to others.

Retraining

Yesterday's skills are inadequate for tomorrow's careers. Studies show that, on average, employees require retraining every five years to maintain their present positions. In five years our work will change dramatically or become obsolete. You will fail if you neglect to retrain to maintain your current position or secure a new one. This is the principal reason why most employees lack security in their professions.

Retraining is not a luxury. Retraining is not optional. It is a matter of survival in our society. It allows us to make easy transitions from one position or career to another. We must not see retraining as something evil or inconvenient. Retraining allows us to prepare for the careers of the future.

Never depend on your employer or others to retrain you. Never assume it is your employer's responsibility to retrain their employees, even though it would benefit them. If your employer has a retraining program make sure they include you in it. Good employers provide free training programs for their best employees. Show your employer you are worth the investment of their time and money.

If your employer does not have a retraining program, ask them to start one. Show your employer it will benefit their company by making them more productive and competitive. It benefits employers when employees can use the latest technology and procedures. These employers will not only retain the best employees, they will also attract the best employees.

Even if your company will not start a retraining scheme, you and other employees can. Do this by sharing ideas, skills and knowledge. Ask employees who are highly skilled in the latest procedures to tutor and train other employees. Use them to teach formal classes.

It is each person's responsibility to develop a personal ongoing training program for themselves. This can include self-study courses, formal classes, and on-the-job training.

Eliminate Negative Thoughts

Our thoughts can guide us to success or to failure. We fail if we lack faith in our abilities. We lose faith because we condition ourselves to fail. Employees become so conditioned to fail they develop techniques to ensure their failure. We allow our fears to paralyze us. We learn to become comfortable as failures because the changes needed to succeed are too risky or require too much effort.

The way to rid ourselves of such limiting thoughts is to change negative beliefs and take action to achieve our goals. Empowering thoughts and persistent actions eliminate limiting thoughts and negative conditioning. Negative conditioning and thinking imprison us and restrict our lives.

In India, they condition baby elephants in this manner: They chain one of their legs to a stake stuck deep in the ground. Because they are not that strong at this early age, the baby elephants are unable to free themselves by breaking the chain or pulling the stick out of the ground. Eventually they stop trying to free themselves. As they grow, unattached chains are placed on the elephant's leg. The elephants are free to leave or wander about, but they never try to walk away. They've become so conditioned to failing they don't even try to free themselves.

In India they catch wild monkeys in an interesting way. Bananas are placed inside bamboo cages. The bamboo bars are placed just far enough apart to allow the monkey's hands to pass through the bars. When the monkey grabs the banana in the cage, it cannot pull its hand back through the bars. The monkey will not let go of the banana to free itself. The hunters come back and capture the monkeys who refused to let the bananas go. The monkeys do not have enough sense to drop the bananas to free themselves. The monkeys do not realize that their freedom is more important than a banana.

Do not behave like monkeys or elephants. Use your ability to think and reason to make good decisions. Never allow your decisions to restrict your capacity to improve yourself or your career.

Develop Sound Working Relationships

Develop good relationships with co-workers by treating them with respect. Give employees credit and rewards for performing well. Never over- or under-reward employees for their work. If you over-reward employees for mediocre performance it encourages substandard work. If you under-reward employees for outstanding work you discourage excellence.

If employees desire more responsibility, give them the chance to grow. When you provide employees with opportunities to better themselves, they become loyal, grateful and supportive. When you exclude employees you restrict your own success. Companies who restrict opportunities for African Americans, other minorities and women are overlooking great resources.

Become a mentor to employees and help guide their careers. Share your knowledge and experience. Help build their confidence and self esteem. Surround yourself with quality people. Select the best candidates. Don't be intimidated by employees who have more experience than you. Use their knowledge. Learn from them.

Take an inventory of yourself and identify changes you need to make. Our working environment has gone through drastic changes. Situations which were unacceptable years ago are now common, such as dating or marrying employees. It's a personal decision whether you date or marry an employee, but in some companies it is detrimental to employees' careers. If you date or marry another employee, conduct yourselves as professionals at work. Don't allow favoritism to affect professional judgment. Do not allow relationships with co-workers to make other employees feel uncomfortable and adversely affect their work.

Always keep work on a professional level. Use professional judgment and common sense before you date or marry a co-worker. It shows poor judgment to jeopardize your career for a one-night stand or two-month fling. Relationships at work can become ugly when they end. With sexual harassment laws, former relationships can become legal issues and grounds for termination. Never allow anyone to use sexual favors to decide their level of advancement or salary increments. This always backfires. It also creates an atmosphere of non-productive work and is the quickest way to the unemployment line. Weigh the pros and cons before making decisions. What appears a sound decision today may be foolish tomorrow. Know company policy on intra-office relationships.

Four Rules for Achieving Permanent Security

Successful people adapt to current market demands. People who adapt to changes in a timely way have security; those who hesitate forfeit theirs. We can take this success formula a giant step forward. Instead of responding to changes, we can implement changes. Permanent security lies in the wisdom not to wait and react to changing environments. It lies in the ability to foresee the future before others and create the changes that others will follow.

Rule #1

Never underestimate your abilities. The greatest inventions and discoveries were not made by corporations. They were made by individual men and women, ordinary people who made their dreams a reality. It was their wisdom, strength, and abilities that created corporations and technological marvels.

Rule #2

Know that being a dreamer is not enough to accomplish the smallest wish. Develop the tools to make it a reality. Be the best and work intelligently. Permanent security is created when we become leaders instead of followers. Instead of waiting for directions, leaders establish their directions and control their outcome. Do not become lax in your actions or attitude. Don't depend on prior success. We must recreate success again and again. This process is what creates unbeatable and unstoppable permanent security.

Rule #3

Never allow yourself to depend on one source for those things that are critical to your success. You are only as secure as the sources available. Fortunes, careers and corporations were lost because so-called reliable suppliers did not keep commitments. Include options in your plans. These options must include alternative sources in case your primary sources become unavailable.

Rule #4

The final rule of permanent career security is to keep current with new trends, and technology. Use new techniques that enhance your abilities. Stay competitive with competitors. Keep abreast of what competitors are doing. Utilize methods that made others successful. If you have no competitors, compete against yourself by establishing goals that make you grow.

* * *

Most people condition themselves to confine their thinking and actions. They see their life as fitting inside a box. They will not venture beyond the confines of the box. This thinking places artificial boundaries around our lives. We must develop the abilities to see and work beyond the boundaries of the box we've created for ourselves and others. This ability is known as "thinking outside of the box." It is an important concept that will ensure your success and establish permanent security in your career.

Chapter 9

Promote Yourself

The best ad is a good product.

—ALAN H. MEYER

PRODUCING superior work is the best form of advertisement for yourself. It is the most effective way to establish a reputation that creates opportunities. The more opportunities we create, the greater our financial rewards, confidence and self esteem.

However, these opportunities will only become available to us if we are recognized for our work. Producing high-quality work contributes little to our success if no one knows about our efforts and accomplishments. Good supervisors and managers acknowledge and reward employees who have put forth extra effort. We do not need a pat on the back for everything we do, but whenever we make major contributions or perform beyond normal expectations, we should be acknowledged.

If you are not receiving deserved recognition, you need to take action. It is not vain or egotistical to seek recognition for your work. It is vital for achieving success. It requires making people outside your immediate circle aware of your capabilities and achievements. They will seek you out to solve their problems.

Most of us are trained to be modest and to avoid bragging about our accomplishments and abilities. Nobody likes a showoff. However, it is important to know the difference between boasting and looking out for your own interests. If you don't learn to blow your own horn, less scrupulous employees will take credit for your work. They often do this if their skills are no longer adequate or inferior to ours. On the surface it appears they are terrible people. In reality they are embarrassed and frightened they will be fired or replaced. They are acting this way to survive, not out of animosity.

Other employees take credit for or discredit your work because they are lazy, or dislike you or what you represent. Some employees hold grudges against fellow employees. They may be for valid or invalid reasons. Employees may dislike you because of something you said, your appearance or dress, or because of your race or religion. They intentionally prevent you from receiving well-deserved recognition or rewards for your efforts.

Others may not dislike you but want to promote someone else. They may want friends or relatives to obtain a position you are competing for. Sometimes employees will intentionally sabotage your work to make you look bad.

Identifying the reasons for conflict is important. Only then can you properly address and eliminate problems. Chapter 10 explains how to resolve conflicts. You will learn skills and techniques to overcome conflicts and how to handle difficult people. In this chapter you will learn how to receive the recognition you deserve.

To resolve the problem of lack of deserved recognition, you must divide it into two separate components. The first is the reason why others are unwilling to give you recognition. The second component consists of strategies to gain recognition even when others are unwilling to give it.

Gaining recognition requires mastering the art of self promotion. If we can eliminate the root of the problem, we will not need to develop an aggressive self-promotion campaign. If we develop a self-promotion campaign without trying to eliminate the underlying problem, we will always be fighting an up-hill battle. We will spend valuable time and energy trying to overcome unnecessary barriers. This is similar to taking medication to treat the symptoms of an illness and never trying to eliminate the cause of the problem. Our illness will never be cured. We will always be forced to deal with the symptoms caused by the illness.

Only if we are unable to resolve the root of the problem will we need to develop an effective self-promotion campaign to gain recognition. Self promotion is nothing more than learning to effectively market and advertise our talents and skills. There is nothing wrong with self promotion when done properly. Companies advertise products. Elected officials and candidates advertise themselves. Successful people are masters at promoting their product — themselves. It is an essential ingredient of their success.

We must create positive impressions when we promote ourselves. We want recognition for the right reasons. We do not want to be known for negative qualities or labeled as problem employees. Never appear tacky or unprofessional when promoting yourself. Do not appear brash, conceited, pushy or obnoxious. Never come across as opportunistic or untrustworthy. If you do, co-workers and managers will not only dislike you, they will sabotage your progress, especially if they think you are placing their positions in jeopardy. Don't become your own worst enemy by alienating co-workers, supervisors and the people you are trying to impress.

Self-Promotion and Marketing Tips

As I said earlier, it is not enough to produce the best work or provide the best services. If no one is aware of your abilities or talents it is unlikely they will think of you when hiring or promoting.

To fix this, start by placing your name and contact information on your work. Do this whether you work for yourself or for a large or small company. If you work for yourself, place your company's name, address and phone number on your work. Include business cards and brochures; they make it easier for customers to contact you. If you work for a company, include your name and department on your work. You can subtly promote yourself by including phrases such as "Prepared by" or "If you have any questions contact [include name, department and phone number]." It is important that people know who you are, what you can do, and how to contact you.

Follow proper protocol. In all organizations there is a chain of command to follow. First, speak with direct supervisors orally and in writing. Your working relationship with your supervisor will determine if they must approve your work before it's released. If your supervisors do not require this, it should be sent to them anyway as a professional courtesy. This is the normal procedure unless there is a formal distribution listing, or a special request for your work. This can be the case when you work on special projects or if a higher authority requests the information. Inform supervisors when this occurs.

Unfortunately, too often our work goes no further than our immediate boss, who may be unwilling to promote it. They often take credit for our hard work. There are several ways to address this problem. First, speak with your direct supervisor in private. Express your concerns professionally. Suggest you are not receiving recognition for your work and feel it will hinder your career growth. If your supervisor agrees and changes the situation, then your problem is resolved.

If your supervisor does not agree, or agrees but does not do anything about it, you must promote yourself. Do this by circulating your name and work without violating the chain of command. Find employees and managers who would benefit from your work. Look for opportunities to meet and speak with them directly. Create opportunities in meetings or by volunteering for committees and organizations in which they participate. Place yourself in situations where they will ask for your input. Find ways to speak or work with them. Send them samples of your work or perform work for them. At meetings or during discussions ask if they would like additional information.

If you don't have the opportunity to ask them personally, try this method: Write a brief note. Base it on conversations, or meetings, or on questions. For example, "I felt this information would be of interest to you." Make sure you sign your name and indicate how you can be contacted. Your brief note makes it appear the recipient solicited your information or you are trying to be helpful.

If for selfish reasons your supervisor does not want you to contact management, think twice before doing so. If you send information that upsets your supervisors, be prepared to accept the consequences. You may be blackballed or fired. Or you may be given a promotion, additional responsibilities, and recognition. Before you take this action, be clear about your objectives. If you are trying to make someone look bad, your actions will backfire. Be concerned about how the reader will react when they receive your information. What will they think of you? Will they appreciate what you did or resent it? Never circulate information for revenge or with malice. If you do, you will end up sabotaging your career.

If you go around your supervisor out of concern for your company or to protect your reputation, it's worth the risk. Your actions may save your career. Timing and seizing the right opportunity is critical to success. Leave the door open for them to request additional information by suggesting you can provide weekly or monthly reports. If they request this information, you just placed yourself in an important loop. You've created a business relationship with important employees other than your boss.

Seek ways to volunteer your services to management. Request additional responsibilities and assignments. This is a great opportunity to showcase your talents and gain recognition. It is also a way of getting around supervisors who will not give you credit for your work. During meetings or conversations individuals may request or refer to information that is not available. Volunteer to do the necessary research. Say you will get back to them with an update. Provide dates and times when you will provide the information or update. and make sure you follow the schedule. Produce quality work that is easy to understand and useful to its intended readers. Prior to starting your work consider the readers' background. The schedule may be considered excellent by the Chief Financial Officer but confusing to the Vice President of Marketing. The intended reader must understand your work in order for it to be meaningful.

Another way to gain recognition is to develop ways to improve the services you provide to others. Ask other employees and departments for suggestions on how you can improve your services to them. If you make recommendations, they must be intelligent ones. Avoid offending others. Don't criticize them or their departments in a way that inflames them, even if it is justified. Do not become offended if you or your departments are justifiably criticized. Use it as an opportunity to turn a negative situation into a positive one. You can make a name for yourself by eliminating problems that others were unable to fix.

If the problems are beyond your scope of authority develop solutions with the appropriate parties. Send them your recommendations for review. Get their input. You may not meet all their needs but maybe you can do something to improve the situation. Even if you do not resolve all the problems, you showed your interest and willingness to help others. You showed others you are willing to work with them and are not their enemy. People will appreciate your efforts and will be grateful you respected their input.

Whenever possible, circulate your work. It must be of high quality and useful to the reader. If your work has no impact on the person you give it to, it has no value. The recipient will not think kindly of you giving them something that is a waste of their time. Your boss has significant impact and control over your future. Never overlook that fact. Try to develop a positive relationship with your boss. Work hard to show him or her in the most positive position. Make your boss comfortable with you and your abilities. Create an atmosphere of trust.

Develop a Reputation

There are many reasons why developing a reputation is important. A good reputation creates unlimited professional and financial opportunities. Developing a positive reputation for yourself both inside and outside your company will also help ensure fair treatment. Good employees often get taken advantage of because their employers know they would have a hard time finding work elsewhere. These same employers will treat employees with well-known reputations better. Such employees are in demand and will have no problems finding new employment.

We can lose our position for reasons beyond our control — companies go bankrupt, plants close down or are relocated, important projects are completed. Having a reputation makes it easier to find new employment. We have an immediate advantage if we are recognized outside our company as valuable employees. In cases of layoffs, downsizing and cost reduction, companies try to keep the employees who have created good reputations. Outside companies recruit individuals with good reputations. Employers make concessions to keep them.

Developing a good reputation is essential for black professionals because of unfounded perceptions. Some believe blacks are lazy, dishonest and unreliable. Many people, including blacks, will not patronize black-owned businesses or hire blacks, and feel uncomfortable working with them because of this false perception. Changing negative attitudes toward blacks is critical to their success.

Minorities and women must not allow invalid perceptions to negatively affect their performance or thinking. All races and genders have honest and reliable professionals as well as incompetent and dishonest ones. Minorities and women perpetuate this problem when they allow subjective thinking and stereotypes to cloud their judgment.

Blacks must accept responsibility for eradicating these false perceptions that they are inferior people. They must eradicate the feeling of being inferior within themselves. This must be done before women and minorities can persuade others to change their negative views. Do this by believing in yourself, thinking and acting like a winner, not like a loser.

Most blacks believe they must be twice as good as non-black employees to be hired or to receive promotions. Often these feelings are justified. Unfortunately, blacks cringe at the thought of being the best. This is definitely the wrong attitude. Blacks should always strive to be the best. Motivate yourself to be the best and create a positive reputation.

It is a wonderful feeling to be the best, but good work alone will not create a well-established reputation. It takes dedication, commitment and hard work. Follow the words of John Burroughs: "For anything worth having, one must pay the price, and the price is always work, patience love, and self-sacrifice." It is essential that you draw positive attention to yourself and your accomplishments to take full advantage of all opportunities. The following are several ways to create opportunities.

Become an Expert

The term "expert" is defined as "a person with a high degree of knowledge or skill in a particular field." It says nothing about how much education or how many degrees you possess. This definition does not mention the color of your skin, your sex or your age. It does not mention how tall, short, fat or skinny you are. Too many of us fail to recognize we possess enough knowledge to classify ourselves as experts. We never allow ourselves to act as experts because we underrate our abilities. If we underrate ourselves no one will accept us as experts.

Just having knowledge and skills is not enough. People make the mistake of acquiring knowledge and skills but never developing the qualities to use them. They look good on paper (education, degrees, work experience) but are unable to produce results.

Putting knowledge and skills to good use requires making the most of what you have. Never dwell on your shortcomings. Develop confidence in your abilities and learn to produce excellent results. Express yourself in a way that shows you are an expert. Keep current with new developments in your field. Show others what you can do. Now you are ready to sell yourself as an expert.

Write Newsletters

Writing newsletters is an excellent way to create exposure and demand for your services. It is an effective way to circulate your name throughout your department, company or industry. You can produce a quality newsletter without spending a fortune. It must be informative, helpful, interesting and professionally done.

With a computer, a word-processing or desktop publishing program, clip art, and a laser printer, you can produce professional newsletters. Most word processing and desktop publishing programs provide newsletter templates. All you need to do is fill in the words.

Start with a catchy name for your newsletter. It must create interest, not turn readers away. Start on a small scale and increase the size and circulation as you gain experience. If you want to produce a company newsletter, obtain proper approval.

There are many benefits to producing a newsletter. It gives you the opportunity to share your knowledge with your readers. It can be a way to meet and interview important people. Learn from people you interview while making important contacts. It will give you excellent experience and increase your value to your employer. This can be the start of an industry-wide reputation.

Write Columns

Another way to develop a reputation is to write a column. A column is a feature article that appears regularly in a periodical. Your column should have a catchy name. It can appear in a newsletter, magazine or newspaper, on a local, regional or national level.

Columns may cover a wide range of topics or be limited to a subject area. They are an excellent way to express views and ideas. If your column relates to your area of expertise, you can showcase your knowledge and abilities.

Columns often allow readers to submit questions. This does not require you to be an expert in all matters. It will require contacting experts or researching questions, providing you with an excellent networking opportunity. You'll be able to approach well-known people by informing them you write a column and require their expertise. Tell them you will give them full credit for answering questions and supplying information. Many experts will do this for the publicity. Writing a column can allow you to have a great impact on public thinking and opinions. It is also a vehicle for making important contacts and creating opportunities.

Write Articles and Editorials

If writing a column is not to your taste or would be too time consuming, writing occasional articles can serve a similar purpose. Unlike columns, articles are not limited to one publication. Query newsletters, newspapers, magazines, trade magazines and journals to publish your articles. You can focus on your field or write about any subject of interest to you.

Writing articles can be an excellent second source of income. It can be done during your spare time. Writing articles adds prestige to your resumé and increases your marketability.

You can also write editorials on important topics. An editorial is an article in a publication expressing the personal opinions of its readers. Articles and editorials will promote your name within and outside your profession.

Write Pamphlets and Books

Writing pamphlets and books is another way to show your expertise. It is also a way to help others and create demand for your services.

Start small and write pamphlets offering career tips. If you do it right you may be able to get your employer to cover your expenses. An example might be a pamphlet for a hospital giving information about their services. If you have an idea for a pamphlet and your employer won't sponsor you, approach other companies or organizations for sponsorship.

If you feel ambitious, write a book. Depending on how well you know your subject, it may require little research. Your first book does not have to be a best seller. Your writing skills improve with each revision and each book you write. Many of us have the knowledge and skills to write excellent books. We never do because we allow our lack of confidence to paralyze us. Let's eliminate the excuses and fears so you can start writing your book today:

- I don't know how to write a book
- I don't know how to have my book published
- I don't have the time or money to write a book

There are excellent books on how to write books. I have listed two of them in the Resources section of this book. They show the most effective ways to write books, how to save aggravation, time and money. Meet with individuals who have written books. Ask them for advice. If you don't know any authors, join writing organizations. There are dozens of them. Find them by using the *Directory of Associations* at your library.

As noted earlier in this book, you can do research without leaving home by using your personal computer. The Internet and CD-ROMs contain huge amounts of data. There are thousands of CD-ROMs available full of information to assist you in your writing.

After you've written your book or articles, you need to know where to sell them. An invaluable resource is the *Writer's Market*. It provides more than 4,000 places to sell your articles and books. This directory provides names and addresses of book and magazine publishers and the subjects they specialize in. It also provides important insights into the business.

Many successful authors did not wait for publishers to publish their books — they published their books themselves. Self-publishing has become acceptable in the publishing industry. Major distributors and book retailers now have small press departments to handle the growing needs of self publishers. There are advantages and rewards to self publishing, along with greater risks and responsibilities. See the Resource section for books on self publishing.

Writing a book requires discipline and the ability to manage your time. You do not have to spend four or five hours a day writing a book. Start by writing one hour a day. Instead of watching TV, talking on the phone or goofing off, invest an hour of this time in writing your book. Consider going to bed one hour later or getting up an hour earlier. Use this extra hour to write your book. Give yourself a reasonable time frame to complete it. Use it to monitor your progress and to adjust writing schedules.

Develop New Technology

Create prestige and recognition by developing new trends and technology in your field. The only thing better than being one of the first to know and use new technology is being the individual who developed it. This creates instant prestige and can result in a fortune for you and others. Those who develop new trends and technologies are considered visionaries. Instead of waiting to react to future developments, they play an important part in defining the future. Instead of following the crowd or playing catch up, they establish the pace for others to follow. Employers and others will pursue you in the hopes that trends and technology you develop will benefit them.

Never fear the idea of developing new technology because you believe it is beyond your capabilities. Not all new technology is as complicated as the phone, computers, micro chips or laser beams. Look at revolutionary new technology as any idea or device that improves the way we live, work or enjoy ourselves. It does not have to be sophisticated or complicated to be effective (i.e., paper clips, Post-It stickers, White-Out, etc.).

Implement New Techniques and Ideas

Never sell you or your ideas short. The importance of new ideas cannot be overstated. God gave us the ability to think. One simple idea can change our lives and our society. A single idea can save a company from disaster and establish you as a major player in your industry. I saved a company from financial ruin with one simple idea that everyone else overlooked. I was hired as the corporate controller for a fast food franchise that had 600 stores. The company was unprofitable and on the brink of bankruptcy. I discovered that about 90 percent of its debt was money borrowed to pay the master leases on time for the 600 franchise stores located in shopping malls. Our company signed the master leases and sublet the locations to our franchises. This made it responsible for paying the monthly rents on time. I discovered we billed the franchises months later, resulting in our negative cash flow.

I also discovered the reason franchisees were billed late. It took months to receive the total charges for each store from the malls. The accounting department waited for all charges for each store location, then billed the franchise for the total charges. I also noticed 90 percent of the charges were fixed while the remaining 10 percent varied each month.

After I discovered this, I came up with an idea to eliminate the need for borrowing money. I decided to bill each franchisee on the fifteenth of the preceding month, instead of months later. This would place the bill in the franchisee's hands 10 days early to ensure we received rent payments in good time. This eliminated the need to borrow money to pay store rents. Since we knew the fixed charges, we estimated the remaining 10 percent. Every quarter we reviewed the variable charges and adjusted the franchisee bills for over or under payments.

Management previously believed that estimating part of the bills was illegal and felt it would create animosity with franchisees. I verified with the legal department that it was legal to bill in this manner. I addressed other concerns by explaining if we did not solve our cash flow problem everyone would lose. The franchisees would lose their investments if the company went out of business. By selling management on the benefits, they quickly supported my idea.

Within six months the company paid off millions of dollars in bank loans and was debt-free. My simple idea saved a company from financial ruin. I was rewarded with a raise, a company car, a year-end bonus, and the respect of management.

Good ideas do not have to be profound. They should not be so complicated that no one except you can understand them. The simpler the idea the better. Good ideas make life easier. They provide benefits and incentives and produce the needed results. A good idea can come from anyone at any time. They have nothing to do with age, position, gender, race, religion or capabilities. Be willing to support good ideas from others. Never allow jealousy to prevent you from supporting good ideas.

Do Volunteer Work

We complain about being unable to obtain positions or start our careers because we lack experience. Many companies are unwilling to hire employees without experience. One effective way to gain experience is volunteer work. It's not always necessary to perform volunteer work in our exact field to gain experience. Many skills are transferable.

Volunteer work also shows employers you are altruistic. This is a quality employers seek in employees. Volunteering shows you care about people and are willing to contribute your time and energy to help others. When performing volunteer work we have opportunities to meet and develop relationships with important people. Best of all, volunteer work makes us feel good about ourselves. Helping others should not be considered an option. It must be viewed as an obligation we look forward to fulfilling.

Be a Teacher

Share your knowledge and experience by teaching others. Never confuse teaching with being a know-it-all. Effective teachers have a desire to help others. You cannot be effective as a teacher if you are using your knowledge to put down co-workers. People know it if you have their interests at heart.

Employers want qualified and talented employees who duplicate themselves by teaching other employees. When you teach others a new skill, they use it to improve the performance of their employer. You gain respect and create demand for your services when you teach others.

The ability to teach is a valuable skill that most people never develop. It takes patience, motivational skills, and a desire to help. Take the time to acquire these skills. Keep current with new trends and developments in your field. Hold informal and organized classes to teach co-workers. Make your lessons informative and interesting. Keep everyone motivated so they benefit from your knowledge. Once you gain confidence, consider leading formal classes and seminars outside your company. Teaching provides valuable experience and exposure.

Public Speaking

Public speaking creates interest in your abilities. It provides the opportunity to display your skills and knowledge. Surveys have shown that many fear public speaking more than death. Most people will do almost anything to avoid speaking in public. They feel uncomfortable speaking with strangers and say little or nothing. As a result, they miss the opportunity let others know what's on their minds.

Developing the skills and confidence to speak in public sets you ahead of the crowd. You'll establish your presence while others go unnoticed. Public speaking is a skill developed by practice. Create opportunities to speak in front of others. Start small — speak in front of friends, then work your way up to speaking in front of larger groups.

Commentary on Television and Radio

Another way of raising your profile is to do commentary segments on television and radio. Broadcasters set aside time for members of the public to express their opinions. Their commentaries may relate to a recent newspaper article or television news story or be a rebuttal to another person's statement or views. As part of government licensing agreements, radio and television stations are required to give the public an allotted amount of free air time to voice their views concerning important public issues. Viewers and listeners can contact these stations and ask to express their comments.

Radio and TV talk shows and panel discussions are always looking for guests. If you have interesting topics and issues to discuss, they may invite you to appear.

If you belong to a professional or industrial association, volunteer to be its media representative. Whenever an event or controversy relating to your field of work arises, journalists may call you up for a quote or to appear on their shows. Being able to handle these sometimes challenging situations with aplomb can make a very positive impression. It is valuable free publicity and exposure, and looks good on resumés and biographies.

Details Make or Break Us

We are judged, rewarded or punished on how well or how poorly we handle small details. They determine how we interact with others. The cumulative effect of how we deal with these seemingly insignificant matters is just as important as the way we handle major responsibilities.

We may produce extraordinary work but display habits or traits that others find offensive. Companies and organizations are conscious of the images employees project. Individuals have lost promotions or were not hired because they displayed poor table manners or lacked social graces during public or business functions.

Always be considerate when dealing with others. If you are a smoker, don't smoke around non-smokers or in their office, home or car. Chewing or loud gum popping is annoying. Consider your tone of voice when you speak. Is it loud, overbearing and offensive? Do you speak too low, does your audience have difficulty hearing you?

Never use offensive language. Never make sexist or racist comments, even in jest. Most individuals do not find them amusing even if they laugh at them. Be careful when discussing religion or politics. Take the time to thank people who were kind and helpful to you. Do you treat others with respect when dealing with them? Do you take the time to learn everyone's name? Do you always smile and greet people in a friendly manner?

Never overlook the importance of personal hygiene and appearance. Unpleasant body odors are offensive and create distance between you and the people you want to impress. Nail biting, fidgeting, or placing your fingers in body cavities (nose, ears, mouth) offends people. Be aware of your actions and how people react to them. Know that some habits are acceptable with certain individuals but are offensive to others. It's impossible to list every situation that offends or annoys others. A course in etiquette may be a worthwhile investment.

Develop good social skills. Combine social skills with common sense and you will have an unbeatable combination. With these qualities you will make the correct impression on others. Strong social skills and common sense can often overcome a lack of experience or knowledge.

Create a Positive Attitude

A positive image is one of your greatest assets. It starts with a positive mental attitude. Nothing makes others notice you more than a positive mental attitude. It's called by different names but it is the common denominator for success in our lives. In Dennis Kimbro's excellent book, *Think and Grow Rich: A Black Choice,* he called it the three magic words — the "right mental attitude." You cannot achieve success without this quality.

A positive mental attitude begins with respecting yourself and others. Employees who possess the right mental attitude are immediately recognized by supervisors and others as outstanding employees. They take control of difficult circumstances.

A survey by the Institute for Enterprise Education (reported in *Profit* magazine, April 1999) asked 40 successful companies which characteristic they considered most important when hiring — attitude, knowledge, or skills. Attitude won by a landslide — 80 percent of respondents said attitude was most important; knowledge was chosen by only five percent, and skills came in last at three percent. Other desired traits were motivation, initiative, responsibility, determination, empathy, confidence and receptivity to change.

Companies value a positive attitude above all because they know from experience that it is what makes the difference between a good employee and a mediocre one. Knowledge and skills are nothing without it.

Professionalism — Do You Have It?

Professionalism is the manifestation of a positive attitude at work. There are many talented and skilled individuals who obtain little success in their careers for one reason: They lack professionalism. Professionalism means professional methods, character and standards we establish for ourselves, and how well we apply them.

In our competitive society one's level of professionalism is often the deciding factor between success and failure. Education and advanced degrees are not enough to make us professionals. Professionalism is not determined just by skills and abilities. We can lack degrees, skills and abilities and still be effective if we have the professional know-how.

Individuals with little experience have started or taken over marginal or failed businesses, then turned them into successful and profitable companies. Their success was determined by the way they conducted themselves. Professionals don't waste their time or energy on counterproductive activities. They address problems in ways that are effective and will improve their situations. They show maturity in their thinking and actions.

They create a positive atmosphere for themselves and others. They avoid petty arguments and idle gossip. They work to bring employees together. They instill the important concept called "team spirit" within them and the individuals they work with. They understand that individual players can accomplish little, while team players working together can achieve the impossible.

Professionals show sound thinking and judgment. They are effective at managing themselves, co-workers, and the individuals who work for them. They make difficult decisions based on facts, not on subjective feelings. They are willing to accept responsibility and show the ability to lead.

Socialize with People
Who Are Different

In our society there is dissension between people because their customs and backgrounds are different. We often bring our biases and irrational fears to work. We allow stereotypes to influence our thinking and behavior. We allow these negative feelings to cloud our good judgment. This creates hurdles that many of us are never able to overcome.

Judge people as individuals and not on preconceived ideas that you and others have. Reserve opinions until you have facts to make objective decisions. Learn to respect the differences in people and not to perceive them as negatives. See others from their point of view and not just yours. Develop interpersonal skills that allow you to get along with others who are different.

Bridge the differences between people and you will have mastered a valuable skill. The ability to get along and to work well with others, regardless of their race, sex, religion or ethnic background, is a critical skill that adds value to employees.

African-American employees should never limit their exposure to black employees. They should seek opportunities to work and socialize with non-black employees. When you only associate with employees of your own race, it demonstrates a weakness in your ability to work with others. You lose valuable learning opportunities and deprive yourself of bridging the gaps between people.

Many problems, hostilities and prejudices we face in our work environment are due to the lack of understanding between people. We can never bridge this gap unless we take the time to learn about each other. Heed the words of Martin Luther King, Jr.: "We must learn to live together as brothers or perish apart as fools." Show your employer you are willing to work to bridge this gap. They will recognize and reward you for your efforts.

Networking

I discussed networking as a job-hunting tool in chapter 3; here I would like to give you some practical tips on networking in a variety of circumstances. Effective networking is one of the best ways to promote yourself.

The key to successful networking is making the most of all situations, regardless of how and when they present themselves. The first rule of networking is to make it fun. We dread meeting people because we see them as strangers or as rude or boring. We become turned off and distant. In reality, our negative thoughts and attitudes turn us into the people we dread meeting. If we change our attitude toward others, we will change the way we think. This attitude change makes it easier to enjoy ourselves when we meet new people. We can change our attitudes by making new rules for ourselves.

Rule #1: Always make networking fun, exciting and beneficial. We can do this by understanding that making new acquaintances provides the best opportunity to make new friends and associates. It is an excellent way to be entertained and to learn new things. Meeting new people is an excellent way to improve ourselves.

Rule #2: Establish advance goals. Know ahead of time what you hope to achieve through networking. Make sure your goals are realistic and reasonable. It takes time to develop meaningful relationships and business contacts — never expect to do this in one meeting. Networks require constant follow-up, exchange of mutual benefits and commitment from all parties. Establish small and large goals for yourself. This will ensure you always achieve some level of success. Develop several plans to achieve your goals. Practice them in trial situations to see how effective they are. Make changes when appropriate, and always strive to improve networking skills.

Rule #3: Be flexible when you meet people. Learn to adapt quickly to different styles and personalities. Recognize and respect the differences in people. This will make it easier for them to enjoy your company.

Follow these additional tips and you will find networking fun, exciting and rewarding:

Never allow your ego to prevent you from taking action, making friends or making the first move. If you spend the evening alone, you will have missed golden opportunities. Approach others and introduce yourself. Re-think your definition of the word "stranger". Instead of seeing a stranger as someone you don't know, see them as potential friends and business contacts.

Understand that most people feel uncomfortable when they first meet. Overcome this problem by developing opening lines to cover this awkward moment. Practice opening lines until you feel comfortable with them. A good laugh puts everyone at ease.

To make conversations worthwhile and interesting, find common interests. Don't limit your conversation to work or your profession. Don't monopolize your audience's time or become loud and overbearing. Allow others to speak and express their views. If you disagree with others' views, don't spend your entire time trying to prove the other party wrong. Use your time to connect with people, not discredit their points of view.

Avoid offensive statements, political views, sexist, and insensitive humor. It shows poor taste and is unprofessional. Avoid them even when others indulge in them. People may not show they are offended but they will remember the incident and hold it against the perpetrator.

If you are going to a function where you don't know people, bring a support team. It will make you feel comfortable having a friendly face around. Make sure you do not spend all your time socializing with your support team. If you do, you will waste the opportunities to make new friends and contacts.

Make the most of every situation. Chance meetings and the way we respond to them can make or break our careers. They can have a profound impact on our personal lives. Be willing to introduce yourself to the president and management of your company. Your conversation may impress them and create opportunities.

Networking can be a simple act of kindness. I experienced this at a party. When my friends and I arrived, a young lady answered the door. She smiled, introduced herself and asked to take our coats. She hung them up and told us to enjoy ourselves. Later that evening I told her how I enjoyed her party. She said she was not giving the party nor did she know the host. I asked her why she had answered the door and hung up our coats. She replied it was the proper thing to do. This one act of kindness created a friendship that has lasted more than 20 years.

We cannot end a discussion on networking without addressing the importance of following up. Follow-up finalizes opportunities. Without it they waste away. Remember to collect and distribute business cards. They are an effective way to advertise your skills and abilities. They are also an easy way for others to contact you. Keep a file for the business cards you collect. You never know when you will need them.

Think Before You Speak

For better or worse, once you've said something, you can never take it back, regardless of how hard you try. Your spoken words will follow you for the rest of your life. If your words are offensive, some people will forgive you, but most will never forget what you said.

Make sure what you say is clear and understandable to your listeners. When your listeners receive a message other than what was intended, you are not communicating effectively. Careers have been ruined because what someone said was not what they meant. Learn to express your thoughts clearly. People fail to realize that effective communication is a specialized skill that requires time and effort to master. Effective communication is essential for success. Your spoken words can work for you or against you. Make your words effective tools that plant the seeds for your success.

The Risk Factor

You probably saw a lot of people on your way to work today. Can you describe everyone you saw? Chances are, you can only describe those people who struck you as different. Their face, clothes, size or actions made them stand out from the crowd.

This holds true in our business and personal life. People notice and remember individuals who are different. We notice and respect people who make changes whether they are successful or not. These individuals are the ones who make an impression on us. They are noticed because they took a risk and broke out of the normal pattern. They didn't follow the crowd; they ended up leading it instead.

Do not sit back and wait for opportunities and chances for success to cross your path. If you do, your life will pass you by while you are waiting for the chance that never comes. Do not blame your lack of success on others because of your failure to use or create opportunities — "The man who said he never had a chance never took a chance."

Don't allow fear to paralyze and prevent you from taking worthwhile risks when you have the best interests of your company and others at heart. Risk-taking is appropriate when you have evaluated all reasonable alternatives and have selected the most appropriate action. Then it is no longer a risk, but a good business decision.

Qualities that Get You Noticed

To close I present a list of some of the qualities I've discussed in this chapter. Have a look at it. How many of these qualities and habits do you possess? Rate yourself. Do you measure up? If you lack any of them, now is the time to develop them. Make them an integral part of you and it will be impossible to go unnoticed.

__ Always prepared   __ Always working

__ Enthusiastic   __ Punctual

__ Always early   __ Completes work

__ Dependable   __ Problem solver

__ Volunteers   __ Shows good judgment

__ Thoughtful

__ Produces results

__ Ethical

__ Empathetic

__ Commitment

__ Leadership

__ Produces quality work

__ Handles stress

__ Needs little or no supervision

__ Does extra work

__ Trustworthy

__ Tactful

__ Superior skills

__ Teacher

__ Professionalism

__ Risk taker

__ Congeniality

__ Positive attitude

Chapter 10

Overcoming
Problems and Conflict

There are two ways of meeting difficulties: You alter the difficulties or you alter yourself meeting them.
— PHYLLIS BOTTOME

If you can't bear no crosses, you can't wear no crown.
— AFRICAN-AMERICAN SPIRITUAL

ONE of life's greatest dilemmas is how to address problems. We usually go about it the wrong way. Rather than address the real root of our problems, we only try to deal with the symptoms caused by them. Lack of effective problem-solving skills is a major reason why individuals fail to find success in their careers and lives.

Unsuccessful individuals rarely take the time to discover what they are doing wrong and the underlying reasons for their problems. They fail to take the necessary steps to correct negative situations. They repeat the same futile actions over and over again, which only produces the same negative results. They fail to realize that repeating ineffective actions never produces satisfactory outcomes.

Many of the problems we experience at work and elsewhere arise from the same source. If we take the time to review difficult situations, we often see a pattern in the types of problems we experience. When things go wrong for us, we may have the same kind of reaction every time. We may say things like, "I just have bad luck"; "Someone's out to get me"; "Why do these things always happen to me?" We may blame others or circumstances for our failure — "Nobody ever listens to me"; "I would've got that job if the subway hadn't made me late for the interview." If we are honest with ourselves, we see that many of our problems are due to our bad habits.

We must learn to master our emotions, develop a positive outlook, and to maintain discipline to achieve our goals. This is the only way we will learn to resolve internal and external problems and conflicts. We cannot exist in our society without encountering problems, so we must develop ways to address them in productive ways.

An effective method for mastering our emotions is to develop beliefs that allow us to deal with our problems. If we adopt the following guidelines, we will establish control over our professional and personal lives.

Guidelines for Improving Your Emotional Lifestyle

- There is no outside emotional stress; there is only my subjective response to a situation, which I can learn to control.
- I will do one thing at a time.
- I will do the best I can about a situation, and then I won't worry about it.
- I will express my feelings honestly to other people.
- I will think and live positively, committing myself to being the best I can be, knowing that even from bad experiences I can learn valuable lessons.
- I will treat all others with the respect I wish for myself.
- I will not feel closed in, but will realize that there are always options.
- I will live in the present and deal with now.

—AUTHOR UNKNOWN

Read these guidelines daily. Ingrain them in your mind. Put them into practice. They will have a dramatic and positive impact on your personal and professional life. This new approach changes the way we think, speak, act and feel. It creates a sense of balance and peace within ourselves. Our effectiveness increases when we learn to prevent problems instead of trying to resolve them as they occur. Most problems are avoidable if we use common sense, control our emotions and take proper actions. We must learn how to calm ourselves when we are in stressful situations. Only then can we address difficulties in a logical and rational manner.

Now let's see how successful people overcome problems and conflicts at work. It does not happen by accident or by luck. They take the time to notice what works for them and others. Equally important, they notice what does not work. They use this information to guide their actions. If they are not obtaining the results they desire, they change their approach.

Let's review common reasons for problems at work. Many individuals allow their anger or egos to prevent them from changing or making adjustments in their life. They become slaves to their anger, pride or egos. When this happens, they are no longer in control of the situation. Never allow anger to control or manipulate you. Uncontrolled anger is often the root of our failures. Make a choice: Is it more important to satisfy your anger or accomplish your goals? Any individual who decides it is more important to satisfy their anger will never achieve success. You may find individuals who fit this category and appear successful. If you examine them closely, though, you will find their success is superficial.

When angry, most individuals' initial responses are hostile verbal ones. Angry verbal responses fail to achieve worthwhile goals. If we want to achieve our goals, first we must learn to control our tongue. Never allow your words to add fuel to a difficult situation. It is more important that we defuse all parties' negative emotions and address the real problems. We must focus on the issues, not satisfying our anger or other emotion. We will never accomplish this if we put our tongues in motion before we put our brains in gear.

Techniques to control your mouth, such as counting to 10 before you speak, usually do not work. Many of us count to 10 as fast as we can and respond in the same manner as if we never counted. We need to take a lesson from Thomas Jefferson: "When angry, count ten before you speak; if very angry, a hundred." We need to give ourselves enough time to calm down, to think and respond rationally.

This is the only way we will improve our situation. It's difficult but the effort will produce results.

The proper response is any that improves your situation. Any response that does not improve your position is not an effective one. Sometimes the best response is one that allows you the opportunity to calm down and collect your thoughts. One way to respond in a confrontational situation is to suggest you need additional time to review facts or figures. You can also respond that you don't have an answer at the moment, then tell them you will get back to them after you have had the opportunity to research the information. When you use these methods, make sure you give a date and time when you will provide the answers. Make sure you honor your agreement.

There will be times when people intentionally put you on the spot to make you angry. They will try to force you to respond in a way that makes you look bad. They will demand an immediate answer when you do not have one. If this happens respond in the following manner: "I have explained to you several times that the information is not available at this time. I've already provided a date and time when I will have a response. Asking me again will not generate any answers and is only wasting our time. Can we move to another topic that will be productive?" Another response might be, "I need a few minutes to refresh my memory. I need to review the data before I can give you an answer. Can I get back to you in a few minutes or a day?" Use the allotted time to obtain an answer and gain control of your anger.

These types of responses will benefit you and others. If you become angry during a meeting, you may want to excuse yourself for a few minutes to calm down. You can always use going to the rest room or leaving to find the information as an excuse.

At other times you may provide a response that someone disagrees with. They may question your abilities or work. This can create anger and tension. Try these methods to gain control of the situation and prevent arguments: Suggest that all parties take a day or so to review the information and schedule another meeting to discuss the findings. This gives everyone the opportunity to calm down and objectively review the situation.

Another method to eliminate counterproductive arguments is to select independent parties to review the facts and determine the appropriate actions to take. Be open to suggestions and solicit comments and recommendations from reliable sources. If someone's idea is better, embrace it. Only by doing this can we use their knowledge and experience to our advantage.

If your idea or approach is ineffective, cut your losses. Accept the fact that we all make mistakes. It is more important to profit from our mistakes than to try to hide them. We profit from mistakes and bad decisions when we learn valuable lessons from them. Never waste your time or energy defending bad ideas or decisions if you know they are wrong or ineffective. When we defend bad ideas or decisions we are really defending our egos or false pride. When we allow this, our thinking becomes subjective. We are unable to make objective decisions.

Another fuel for our anger is the rules we establish for ourselves and others. When people act contrary to our rules, we become upset and angry. The violation of rules we establish for others is probably the primary reason for conflict in our social and professional lives.

We cannot live in a society without laws and rules. We need them to establish order. They allow individuals in a society to function together. Without rules in our lives there would be chaos. Rules are established to create order, harmony and continuity in our society. We must also develop and abide by rules we establish for ourselves.

The problem is that many of the rules we devise and apply to others are ineffective, foolish, and meaningless. Instead of creating harmony, stability and order in our lives, they create anger, confusion, frustration, and chaos. Often the individual rules we bring to work are based on personal taste, customs, and experiences. They have nothing to do with creating order or promoting harmony in our working environment.

Here's an example: The owner and president of a small company had developed a personal "rule" that he always had to win arguments. He would go to any length to make others admit he was right. He would even provoke arguments for the sole purpose of crushing his opponents. Needless to say, it wasn't very pleasant to work for this man. The confrontational atmosphere his personal rule created led to frequent turnovers in his staff. He lost valuable employees because he focused on winning senseless arguments with them rather than hearing their valid suggestions for improving the company.

Such rules have no rational basis. They arise out of our unconscious needs and reactions to events in our lives. They only reveal their existence when we stop to figure out why we keep having the same kinds of problems over and over again. The man described in the example above attributed his high staff turnover to outside factors. He has never considered whether his own behavior might be a cause, because his rule has become an integral part of himself.

Everybody has these kinds of harmful rules. Once we acknowledge this fact, we can work to change them. We can consciously devise rules that work for us, not against us. This book was not written to define your personal rules. It would be inappropriate for others to establish personal rules for you to live by. To assist you in establishing your personal rules use these guidelines when developing them:

- Establish rules that improve others' lives as well as yours.
- Establish rules that provide long-term benefits.
- Never establish superficial or fashionable rules to become popular. Their benefits never last.
- Evaluate your rules to improve them and to determine if they are working. Eliminate inappropriate rules that are the source of your failures.
- Create rules that allow you the flexibility to address problems you will encounter in your work environment.
- Create rules that allow you to pick the time and place to make a stand as well as the option to overlook situations when it is in your best interest. Winning an unimportant argument at the expense of being terminated shows poor judgment.

- Never make insignificant situations major catastrophes. Isolated incidents should be treated as isolated incidents. They should never be globalized ("this always happens"). Don't internalize problems.

- Accept reality — life is not always fair. Good does not always win over evil. Bad things happen to good people. People who commit evil deeds go unpunished. When you dwell on what people did, you are only punishing yourself. Focus on making the future better, not on avenging the past.

Take the time to establish rules that add value to your life. Write them down and commit them to memory. Make a commitment to follow your rules. If they are not working, adjust them. Use your rules to guide decisions and actions. Once you develop appropriate rules, it's difficult for situations to trigger destructive feelings and emotions. This gives you great power in your work environment.

Overcoming Adversity

Believing that even the best rules will prevent us from experiencing adversity and emotional turmoil in our careers is foolish. Going through life without experiencing conflict and emotional distress is impossible. Negative emotions will destroy us unless we turn them into a positive force.

We can turn adversity into a positive experience when we acknowledge life is not always fair. Things happen for a reason. We always have options. In fact it is important that we periodically experience conflict and emotional turmoil in our lives because "Adversity introduces a man to himself" (Anonymous). When we properly use adversity, it becomes beneficial. This happens when we use anger to enrich our lives. We can never accomplish this if our actions are based on revenge and hate.

Look for ways to turn negative situations into positive ones. If you did not get a promotion due to lack of skills or education, use this as a catalyst to obtain the skills or education you need. If you were denied a promotion for unfair reasons, consider starting your own business or working where there are more opportunities.

Never allow adversity to destroy your life. To improve your circumstances, you need to take a serious and objective inventory of yourself. Often this self inventory will be painful and depressing. You may come to realize you are not properly using your talents or not putting forth a sincere effort to succeed. Acknowledge the skills and education you are missing, but don't dwell on your lacking them. This will only depress you. Instead, focus on the abilities you do have that will allow you to obtain the skills and education you need. Too many individuals fail because they allow adversity to defeat them and give up. This guarantees failure. Whenever you feel like giving up, remember the words of Helen Keller: "Never bend your head, always hold it high. Look the world straight in the face." See adversity for what it is: the opportunity to improve our lives and the lives of others.

When others win first place or receive all the accolades, it does not diminish your value as a human being. Stop believing you must always win or garner all the spoils of victory. This "win all or nothing" attitude can be fatal. It takes the enjoyment out of your life. Never stop striving for the best. Take time to savor the small wins during the process of achieving success. Appreciate the lessons you receive from your failures. Realize the sum of the small wins and the lessons you learn from past failures is success.

The Art of Making People Want to Change

Conflicts start between co-workers, supervisors, and subordinates when each party tries to change the other's thinking or behavior. Each side sees the other side as unwilling to change and being difficult. This is another source of arguments, ill feelings, misunderstandings and problems at work. We waste far too much time trying to change individuals who are unwilling to change.

Most of the common ways we try to get others to do what we want them to do are ineffective. We try to intimidate others into doing what we want them to do. We threaten them with disciplinary action, loss of pay or loss of employment. We holler and scream at them and ridicule their ideas. These tactics may force individuals to do what we want, but it also creates animosity toward us. This resentment is the source of conflict in our working relationship. Long after the project is done, these individuals will carry ill feelings toward you.

We will get better results if we change the way we treat others. Simply by altering our approach we can get individuals to change willingly. We can start by not treating everyone the same. Most of us have one or two approaches that we use for everyone. Take the time to learn about the people you are dealing with. Treat them as individuals. Learn their needs, likes, dislikes and the level of their abilities. Understand the reasons for their objections. They may be valid or something we can overcome quickly.

Too many of us feel that if someone disagrees with us or is hesitant to do what we want, they are the enemy and should be treated as such. When this happens, we set ourselves up for ongoing conflicts with others. We need to take the time to investigate the reasons for their lack of cooperation. We need to try to overcome their objections.

Let's look at some reasons why others may disagree with our ideas:

- They fear change.
- They fear they are unable to perform the task.
- They lack the abilities to perform the work.
- We did not create energy and excitement for our ideas.
- We did a poor job selling our ideas.
- They lack confidence in our abilities and our ideas.
- They don't trust us.
- We offended them.

- They harbor personal prejudices against us.
- They fear we will take their position.
- They are not aware of the benefits they will receive.

Fearing change is common. People find comfort in familiarity. They panic when they are forced to face the unknown. To help individuals overcome their fears be sensitive to not only their questions but their objections as well. Spend time making people comfortable with your ideas. Don't become annoyed if they ask questions; be willing to answer them. They are trying to learn or quiet their fears.

Many fear they cannot master new ideas and procedures, or worry they will be too slow learning them. Assure people they will be properly trained. Realize some learn faster than others. Provide sufficient time for employees to learn and master new skills. Provide written, oral and visual training that is thorough and easy to follow. Make it fun and informative.

Assign employees to positions and areas of responsibility that meet their skill levels. You can have the greatest idea in the world, but it will not be implemented if you assign individuals who do not possess the abilities to perform the duties. You cannot train an employee for a position that is beyond their capabilities. They will become frustrated and end up resenting you and your ideas. This is also true in reverse: Never place over-qualified employees in positions that offer little challenge. They will become bored and unhappy.

Show your enthusiasm and passion for your ideas and projects. If you don't, neither will anyone else. It is your responsibility to create energy and excitement for your project. Make sure your enthusiasm becomes contagious. This is how you create support for your projects. Take the time to explain and sell important ideas or projects. If you cannot sell them, you will never convince others to support you. Don't think because your ideas or projects are excellent people will immediately embrace them. Many great ideas never become reality because sponsors do a poor job selling them. It is normal for people to be skeptical when they are presented with new ideas. An important part of your sales presentation is to make others comfortable about your ideas or projects.

In many situations others will not support you because they lack confidence in your abilities. No one wants to join a losing team or waste their valuable time. Inspire confidence in your skills and abilities by completing all work assignments, by being dependable, and by honoring your word. Show that you are committed to your work.

It is essential that we master the skills of persuasion. Persuading individuals to support us is more effective than forcing them to do something against their will. When we force others to support us, they resent us. Whenever they have the opportunity to avenge their sense of injustice they will jump at the opportunity. When we persuade individuals to support our ideas or actions, they willingly support us because we've shown them it is in their best interest to do so. This eliminates resentment or hostilities toward us.

It is important to develop trust between our supervisors, subordinates, co-workers and others whose support we require. Trust is not something automatically given or received. Trust is not created by position, level of education or abilities. Trust is a quality earned by past deeds and actions. Show others they can rely upon you to keep your commitments. Never make commitments or give your word if you have no intention of honoring them.

People will harbor ill feelings against you if they feel you offended them. You may have offended employees unintentionally. Many employees will never mention this but will carry a grudge against you. You will notice they act unfriendly or are distant toward you. Be sensitive to people's feelings and actions. Take the initiative in addressing these types of problems. Accept the responsibility to create positive dialogue between you and others. This is the first step toward overcoming differences or ill feelings toward you.

Some individuals resent good ideas and projects because they fear they will make them look incompetent and eventually you or someone will replace them. To eliminate this fear, include them in the planning stage and make sure they receive credit. Be recognized as the lead person on a project, but share credit with others.

The nature of progress is change. It is a fact that many good ideas eliminate old positions or change them drastically. Be honest with employees. Don't tell them your proposal will not affect their position when it will. Show compassion to individuals who may be terminated. Help them find new employment. Where possible, retrain employees for new positions within your company. Employers cannot afford to keep unproductive employees on the payroll, but turning them into productive employees is less costly than severance packages. It creates good will and employee loyalty, which are beneficial to the company.

As discussed earlier, people will not change their attitudes unless they want to change. Fear, force, and intimidation are not effective tools for getting people to support you. They only create additional conflict. The best way to get individuals to change is to show them it is in their best interest to change. Another way to eliminate their fears is to share knowledge. When you teach others, they gain confidence. Through their newfound confidence they no longer fear you. They will also be supportive of your ideas and be willing to help you implement them. You will develop a bond with these employees. Through this bond you will gain their trust and admiration.

Make employees aware of the benefits they will receive if they are willing to change their attitudes. Show how your ideas will make their work easier, more productive, profitable, and increase their chances for advancement. You cannot accomplish this if your ideas or projects are of poor quality. Your first step in accomplishing this task is to start with good ideas that will benefit others.

Misery Loves Company

A constant source of aggravation at work are employees who are always miserable. They always have a sad story. They are always willing to dump their problems on others. Some people love being miserable. They feel comfortable when they are miserable. It is their way to gain attention, or to get out of doing their work, or to avoid accepting responsibility. Some people have deeper problems they don't want to address. Being negative and miserable has become their way of dealing with them. It's become a habit with them and they don't have the energy or emotional strength to change. They want others to feel their misery and pain because it reassures them.

We all experience problems. There is nothing wrong with helping employees, as long as they are not taking advantage of you and others. Beware of employees who always have problems and are unwilling to address or resolve them. These employees are constantly whining, complaining and looking for sympathy. They make sure everyone is aware of their problems. They spread this form of poison and have a negative effect on you and others. They will do anything to make you feel sorry for them. They seek sympathy by making others feel guilty.

Never allow yourself to feel responsible for these types of people, especially if they are unwilling to help themselves. These individuals are often the source of office gossip, arguments and ill feelings. Only associate with these employees when you have to. If you must work with them, be careful what you say and do in front of them. These individuals are often experts at making friends and gaining others' confidence. They will use whatever you tell them against you to improve their position. They often do small favors (whether asked for or not) to make you feel obligated toward them. In return they expect you to be indebted to them for life.

Try to get along with others but know it is impossible to be friends with everyone. No matter how hard you try, you cannot please everybody. Be careful when choosing the employees you will work with. Sometimes we are forced to work with employees we do not trust or respect. They are unwilling to do their share. Make sure responsibilities are clearly defined. By doing this, you can show you are only accountable for your share of the work.

Fear of Failure

In the beginning of this chapter we stated the greatest problems and conflicts are often with ourselves. They are not problems created by others. The fear of failure is the greatest conflict most of us face in our professional careers. We allow this fear to prevent us from taking proper actions to improve our prospects. We allow this fear to paralyze us.

To eliminate this internal conflict we must develop philosophies that empower us and eliminate our fears. Start by reading this quotation:

> *I don't care how much a man may consider himself a failure, I believe in him, for he can change the thing that is wrong in his life any time he is ready and prepared to do it. Whenever he develops the desire, he can take away from his life the thing that is defeating it. The capacity for reformation and change lies within.*
>
> —PRESTO BRIDLE

Let's make this quotation even more powerful for us. We can do this by making it personal and committing ourselves to its tenets:

> *I believe in myself, for I can change the thing that is wrong in my life any time I am ready and prepared to do it. Whenever I develop the desire, I can take away from my life the things that are defeating it. The capacity for reformation and change lies within. I am committed to make the change today.*

Memorize this quotation and repeat it out loud whenever you feel like giving up. It will restore your confidence.

Avoid Arguments

Many arguments we experience are avoidable. It only requires a willingness to develop the skills to foresee potential problems before they occur. We must then take the necessary steps to avoid them.

Arguments occur because someone's ideas or thinking is different from ours. Because we are not familiar with them, we feel uncomfortable or threatened. Just because ideas are different does not mean they are right or wrong; it only means they are different. Maintain an open mind when you are presented with new or different ideas. Don't allow subjective thinking to prevent you from learning new concepts. Learn to value and respect other people's judgment and opinions. Do not make hasty decisions. Be willing to learn from others regardless of their position or status. Evaluate and research other people's ideas before you make judgments.

Take the time to listen to what others are saying. Most arguments occur because one or more of the participants are not listening, only waiting for their turn to speak. They never show interest in what the other party has to say. This creates communication barriers that prevent participants from reaching agreement.

Show respect for others when they speak. Allow others to express their ideas without cutting them off. Give the speaker your full attention. If you do not agree with others' ideas, do not try to ridicule or embarrass them. If you do, they will never be receptive to your ideas. Instead they will try to get revenge by trying to embarrass or ridicule your ideas in turn.

If you do not agree with others' ideas, take the time to explain why you cannot support them. Make sure your reasons are legitimate. They will see right through invalid excuses. They will lose respect for you because of your dishonesty. This will only set the stage for future disagreements and confrontations. Be honest and open with others and they will respect you for it.

When presenting ideas to others be sensitive to their differences. Try to understand their current situations, customs, and experiences. Determine the best way to approach them to overcome any concerns they have. Use influential people to help you achieve your objectives. Arguments are often created not by conflicting opinions, but by conflicting personalities. Learn to move past the differences in personalities. Address issues, not personalities. Smile, act cordial, and apologize to others even when you do not want to. Be sincere or you will only make matters worse.

In order for others to buy into your ideas, eliminate potential arguments. Gain your peers' and supervisors' confidence. Disagreements start because your peers or superiors do not respect you or your abilities. They base their opinions on how you conduct yourself, your past actions and accomplishments. Do you honor your word? Do you accept responsibility? Can you be trusted? Are you dependable? Take the necessary steps to gain the respect and trust of your peers and supervisors. Without respect your peers and supervisors will not support you or your ideas, even when they are excellent ones.

What to Do During an Argument

During arguments, never focus on satisfying your emotions. Allowing your anger to control you will distract you and drain your energy. It will cloud your judgment and prevent you from resolving the real issues. Focus on resolving the problem, not satisfying your ego, emotions or sense of justice.

The best way to address arguments is to prevent them. It is impossible to eliminate all arguments, but we can take actions to reduce them or minimize anger. We can avoid or minimize arguments by the way we respond to others' actions and the way we address them. First, carefully select the most appropriate response. Identify what you want to accomplish, then identify which response will accomplish your goal. No matter what your responses, review the results. A response only works when it accomplishes the goals you desire. If it does not, change it. Remember that a response may work in certain situations but not in others. Your response is determined by the individuals you are addressing and the related circumstances. Always tailor your response to get the best results from the parties involved. Now let's review some appropriate responses.

Ignore or Respond?

We can determine if we should respond to or ignore comments or actions by following these rules: When it is in our best interest to ignore comments or actions, ignore them. When it is in our best interest to respond, we must respond.

During our career we will meet adversaries whose only goals are to make us upset, look bad, or harm our position. They do this by trying to make us lose our composure. They try to bait us into senseless arguments. If we fall into this trap we lose our focus and are unable to accomplish our goals. If someone makes trivial comments or small insults, try ignoring them. Determine if it is appropriate by asking this question: Is it more important to respond to inappropriate comments or actions or is it more important to accomplish my primary goal? If your answer is objective, you will always make the right choice. Ignoring individuals will often make them look bad and make you appear professional.

We must respond to trivial comments or actions if they become destructive and interfere with our goals. When we respond, we must do it in a way that helps us to achieve our goals, not to satisfy our emotions. When possible find the real reason for their actions and address them. Distinguish between legitimate questions and issues, and phony ones. Always respond to legitimate concerns, even when they appear trivial. Make sure your response is well thought out. If you choose not to ignore what someone said or did, carefully pick the best time and place to respond. Do it at a time and place that puts your opponent at a disadvantage.

Neutralize Your Opponent's Objections

If we try to ignore objections, our opponents will escalate their objections. The way to neutralize objections is to acknowledge legitimate issues and take the necessary steps to eliminate or minimize them. Work with concerned parties to address any objections they have. Often your opponent will accept your ideas if you just acknowledge their issues, even if their concerns are not eliminated. They feel better because you've taken the time to acknowledge them and showed an interest in what they said.

Try not to discredit or make an opponent look bad unless it cannot be avoided. This only escalates opposition, arguments and ill feelings. Do your homework. Know what the objections are. This allows you the opportunity to resolve issues before they become issues. Occasionally you may be unable or unwilling to overcome objections; for example, the cost may prohibit you from taking the actions needed to eliminate the objection. The objection's disadvantages outweigh its advantages. Point out these disadvantages to persuade others to drop their objections. Often an objection is not related to your ideas. Table these types of objections as side issues which should be addressed later. Suggest you will be glad to discuss these or other non-related issues in private or after the meeting.

Put Them on the Defensive

Putting others on the defensive may eliminate their immediate objections but it creates the seed for future confrontations. Avoid creating situations where you place others in a position where they have to defend themselves. When others feel they are attacked they will criticize you in return.

Only put on the defensive individuals who are injuring you, your position or others. Do this as a last resort after you have exhausted all other options to get your point across. Don't do it merely to make others look bad. Place opponents on the defensive by showing why their ideas will not work. Provide facts, statistics, charts and schedules to prove your point.

If you are forced to put someone on the defensive, make sure you follow these rules: To eliminate or reduce future animosities, always allow your adversary opportunities to gracefully bow out of uncomfortable situations. Never block an opponent's way to exit an uncomfortable situation with dignity. If you do, you will force them to escalate their objections against you to save face or get out of the situation.

Win Them Over

Winning your opposition's confidence and support is the most effective way to eliminate arguments and disagreement. Whenever you can persuade your opposition to willingly change their ideas, you not only eliminate obstacles you also create support.

The best way to win others over is to show them it is in their best interest to support your ideas and actions. Start by showing them the benefits they will receive. Show them how it will improve their current position and create opportunities for them. It is important that the benefits be real. Never promise anything you cannot provide. Never make exaggerated claims or statements.

Another method for winning others over is humor. Humor can reduce anxiety in a tense atmosphere. Introducing humor into tense situations helps eliminate differences and places individuals at ease. It allows individuals to let their guard down and to be open to suggestions.

Compromise

When at an impasse, be willing to negotiate. First, identify priorities. Next, identify what you will and will not give up. Then identify what benefits you have and are willing to offer to entice others to support your ideas. Offer something that is of value to the other parties involved. Develop a relationship of mutual value and cooperation. Consider all alternatives. Be flexible in your thinking.

Rethink your ideas and admit mistakes. Cut your losses when it is appropriate. Accept the ideas and recommendations of others when they are in your best interest. To accomplish your goals, you may have to retreat or adjust your time table until the time and place are more conducive to your success.

How to End an Argument Effectively

The way we end an argument determines if it will improve our situation or hurt it. To ensure an argument provides value, end it in one or more of the following ways:

Do not make meaningless threats. If you do, people will see through them. They will ignore what you have said because they've lost respect for you. Establish a bottom line that empowers you and provides choices. It is the final action you will take to resolve the problem. Often we lose something when we resort to our bottom line. Be willing to accept the consequences associated with your decisions. Exchanging minor losses for major gains is smart.

If you lose more than you gain, your bottom line is ineffective. Informing your boss you will quit the next time you are treated unfairly is not a worthwhile benefit if you find yourself unemployed and unable to support your family. A more effective bottom line would be to look for new employment and resign after you find it.

Avoid senseless arguments. They are a waste of time and increase your aggravation. Don't focus on having the last word. Trying to have the last word only prolongs arguments. It makes you look foolish, demonstrates a lack of control, and alienates others.

End arguments on your strongest point and with an important message. Don't end arguments by focusing on anger or revenge. End them with the intent of resolving problems. It does not help to continue to argue when you have reached an impasse and important issues are unresolved. Take it to a higher source for final resolution.

Be objective when others have legitimate concerns. Work to eliminate or minimize objections identified during arguments. Don't become offended when others question your ideas.

Find your opponents' real issues and their price to resolve them. Often others do not have problems with our ideas. Their opposition stems from unrelated issues. Find the real issues and overcome them.

Feuds

The only thing worse than an irrelevant and unproductive argument is a foolish, ongoing feud. It is not important how it got started or who gets the last word in. The important thing is to quickly and effectively end it. Feuds between rivals only end when all parties can put their past behind them. Only then can they begin to work in harmony. Harmony means there is no desire for revenge or ill feelings toward others.

Feuds are perpetuated by the internal anger and the grief we carry. This grief is based not only on the actions of others but our actions as well. During feuds we demand revenge to satisfy our sense of justice. For each offense there is a retaliatory action by the offended party. This situation perpetuates feuds into never-ending cycles.

In the work place, the impact of feuds is compounded because innocent employees are often forced to choose sides and are dragged into battles as unwilling participants. Innocent victims are often casualties of feuds. Feuds cause us to lose sight of the real issues at hand. They prevent us from accomplishing our goals.

Regardless of how long feuds have existed, they can be eliminated when good judgment prevails. There is the story of Willie Brown, former Democratic California State Speaker of the Assembly, and the legendary feud he had with five Assembly members. The feud was so intense Brown's five adversaries were nicknamed the "Gang of Five". For years they tried to remove Brown from office. This feud was public and detrimental to the citizens of California. Brown eventually defeated the Gang and stripped them of their power.

Shortly thereafter, Willie Brown did something that appeared foolish: He appointed one of the Gang of Five to a powerful position. When asked why he helped his former adversary, he replied that he would rather create an ally than an enemy. Baltasar Gracin explained it this way: "A wise man gets more use from his enemies than a fool from his friends."

Ending feuds requires a willingness to forgive others and yourself for past actions. Be willing to make concessions and gestures of good faith. Good-faith gestures must be respected or future relationships will be jeopardized. Explain what you expect and know what is expected of you. Don't become upset with others if they disagree with you. Establish new rules that all parties are comfortable with and agree to freely. Be committed to preventing future feuds. This requires overcoming small and important issues before they become serious. Be objective, diplomatic and flexible.

Conflict Management

Who is the better manager of people —

> the professional who recognizes potential conflicts between others, then quickly and effectively defuses them before they become problems

OR

> the professional who willingly overcomes conflicts with others, regardless of how long it takes, how difficult it is, or how battered they become in the process.

Prevention (the first method) is by far the most effective method for eliminating conflict. Your success is determined by how and where you expend your time and energy. Spending your time fighting or resolving conflict is counterproductive. Dealing with conflicts often leaves us so battered we are unable to properly perform our normal duties. Unless they are professional fighters, people who come to work looking for a fight have serious problems.

Regardless of how effective a manager you are, there will be situations when you will be in conflict with others. When you find yourself in this situation follow these simple rules:

Your level of defense must not be in excess. If an employee makes an unflattering comment, do not overreact. It is not an appropriate use of your time and energy feuding or arguing with that person because of a small meaningless incident.

Your level of defense must not be inadequate. If it is, employees will feel the benefits exceed their punishment. This encourages employees to continue their actions. If an employee intentionally sabotages your work, your response must adequately reflect the level of offense. Appropriate responses are termination, suspension, or final warning. If you lack the authority to take action, refer these infractions to the appropriate parties.

When you are at an impasse, appoint a mediator to resolve conflicts. Select a neutral person who will objectively review the matter. All parties must agree to abide by the mediator's decision. If you want to be a successful manager, develop the skills to properly mediate and resolve problems between employees, customers and suppliers.

Your level of response is critical. It will serve notice that you will act accordingly to match an offense. Otherwise, you will allow others to take advantage of you. Your response must never be one that advances your adversary's causes. Choose your response carefully. Your actions will determine how others treat you.

Working with Employees You Don't Like

In our professional and social lives we often become too judgmental. We place too much emphasis on whether we like certain people and not enough on whether they can they be instrumental in helping us accomplish our goals. We commonly steer clear of individuals we don't like in order to satisfy our emotional sense of dislike for them. This is an emotional decision based on inappropriate thinking. We may not like their appearance, the way they walk, their manner of dress. We may not like the way they speak, where they were born, where they come from or where they live. We may not like their religion, race, customs or social status. We may be jealous or envious of them.

Such dislikes usually arise from our own insecurities. Not only is it unfair, but avoiding or ignoring people for these personal, irrational reasons is often counterproductive. These people may have much to offer. Your decision to avoid others for petty or irresponsible reasons eliminates valuable opportunities. No law or rule states you cannot make major accomplishments by working with someone you dislike. Focus on achieving important goals and what you can accomplish, not on your emotions and subjective opinions.

Good working relationships are valuable, but they do not require we develop friendships or bonds with co-workers. Nor does it mean we must socialize with co-workers outside work. It does require that we respect each other's abilities and potential. When we work together we must value and support each other's work. When we do this, our differences start to magically disappear. Sometimes close bonds and friendships are forged.

Initiate honest dialog with co-workers who are different or loners. Communication eliminates differences between us. It creates understanding and compassion for our differences.

Working with a Difficult Boss

Always remember this when dealing with your boss: The boss may not always be right, but he is always your boss. The nature of a boss's responsibilities places him or her in a position of authority and power. There will be times when we disagree with our bosses. We should respect their opinions even when they are different than ours. Fully understand their reasons. Ask for clarification and listen to them objectively to ensure understanding. Ask yourself if their reasons are better than yours.

If you still disagree with your boss, politely and respectfully explain your position. If your boss does not agree with you, do not act disrespectful. It may be best to go along with your boss even when you disagree. This is always true for minor differences.

There are situations when it is not appropriate to support or agree with your boss, such as when your boss's actions are in direct conflict with your principles. For example if your boss requests you to do something unethical, immoral or illegal, or that places you or others in danger, you must stand your ground.

If you must disagree with your boss, use the following guidelines to reduce or eliminate current or future conflict and to protect yourself:

- Always show respect for your boss. If you can't respect your boss as a person, respect his or her authority and position.

- Do not try to make him or her look bad. If you disagree with your boss, do it with the intention of improving a situation, not being malicious.

- Do it to show a different viewpoint and to introduce important ideas or information that may have been overlooked.

- Have all the facts. Know what you are talking about. Know both the advantages and disadvantages of your ideas.

- Do it for important issues. Weigh the pros and cons before you decide to force an issue.

- If you confront your boss, do not force him or her into a corner. Provide choices that allow you and your boss empowering alternatives.

Select an appropriate time and place for your discussion. Make sure each of you has sufficient time to discuss the issues. Select a place that is comfortable for you and your boss. Don't disagree with your boss in front of others. He or she may feel it is more important to defend their ego or reputation than to address the issue.

If the situation is one that is unethical, illegal or that would have a catastrophic impact on the company, you need to inform someone with the authority to investigate and resolve the matter. If you fail to do this you may be held responsible and your career ruined. It can even lead to legal problems and financial losses.

Never approach your boss when you are upset. If you must say something, just inform your boss you are upset and would like to discuss your concerns with him or her after you calm down. Schedule a date, time and place where you can meet.

Realize there are bosses who will not accept the truth regardless of how well it is presented to them. This is their problem, not yours. Good only always wins in the movies — that's a reality. Be willing to lose some battles to win the war. Be willing to give up something small to gain large rewards. Learning to compromise is your key to success.

Dealing with Discrimination

In my book, *Breaking the Glass Ceiling: Sexism and Racism in Corporate America*, I showed how discrimination against minorities and women persists in the corporate world. The term "Glass Ceiling" was coined to describe the invisible, artificial barrier that prevents minorities and women from rising in the work place. Studies and recommendations have been made by government departments and non-profit organizations to eliminate these discriminatory practices. They have helped to publicize the daily problems minorities and women face in the work place.

As important as they are, we cannot depend on the government, companies or organizations alone to eliminate this problem. All minorities and non-minorities, men and women, must be willing to address this problem. The only way to eliminate discrimination is to show companies it is in their best interest to change and develop new philosophies.

We must show companies how counterproductive it is to discriminate against minority and women employees. In our current economic climate we need to utilize all the resources (employees) available. Our markets have become global and extremely competitive. Successful companies see and use diversity as an asset and opportunity to increase their markets and profits. It allows them to be sensitive to the needs of their diverse customers.

Old beliefs and practices such as discrimination are no longer profitable. Local businesses must be sensitive to the communities they serve and the employees who serve them. Business can no longer take from the community without giving something back. Businesses must be concerned about the public image and reputation they create for themselves. This starts with the relationship they build with their employees.

Discriminatory practices reduce the quality and quantity of work. They create negative atmospheres that adversely affect employees' attitudes and creativity. Companies are living entities. They can only survive by allowing the roots (employees) to be properly nurtured. When we cut and starve the roots (minority employees) we weaken the whole organism. Once this happens companies lose vital strength and the stability needed to survive. This happens when we unfairly restrict the growth of qualified minority and female employees.

There is another drawback to discriminating against minorities and women: If discrimination against one class or race of people is permitted, it becomes easier to discriminate against others. These same companies allow discrimination on the basis of sex, religion, ages, appearance and other attributes. Once this happens a fatal cancer spreads throughout the company.

The most effective way to combat discrimination is to show employers it is not in their best interest to practice or tolerate it. Show employers that eliminating this practice improves their company's performance. When addressing this problem, approach co-workers or employers with an attitude of fellowship, not hostility. Be sincere and firm when addressing this issue. Share this thought with them:

> *We must learn to live together as brothers or perish together as fools.*
> —MARTIN LUTHER KING, JR.

Some employees and companies are unwilling to listen or accept the truth. When you address this problem, be willing to accept the consequences. If they are not receptive, you can experience serious repercussions. Plan your approach wisely and prepare for a worst-case scenario. Have options available in case the situation is not resolved. There are risks but the rewards far outweigh them. If you address discrimination properly, you will open the doors of opportunity. Never wait for others to address this problem because of fear or excuses. "If you are not part of the solution you are part of the problem." Take the first step to improve your and other minorities' career opportunities. Remember the Chinese proverb: "A journey of a thousand miles must begin with a single step."

This prospect appears too frightening to most of us. We've all heard horror stories about individuals who unsuccessfully tried to address these problems at their place of employment and how they suffered for their efforts. We must not focus on the failures of others but on the individuals who were successful and profited from their efforts. This number is growing larger each day. These individuals are people of character who showed courage and moral conviction.

To be successful in our endeavors, it requires new attitudes and innovative approaches. Do not focus on the horror of the past but on the rich opportunities of the future available when we challenge ourselves. I like the approach that cognitive therapy uses. It was developed more than 20 years ago by Dr. Arron T. Beck, at the University of Pennsylvania School of Medicine. Dr. Beck developed mood-elevating techniques that were different from the traditional methods used to treat blue moods and depression, and to help us feel good about our lives. Traditional methods involved analyzing past problems over and over again to determine how they mentally scarred us. This often took years of painful therapy and soul searching.

Dr. Beck felt that reliving negative experiences over and over again made us feel worse and increased our problems. Instead, he decided we should address problems from a new viewpoint. This requires changing our thinking process and taking immediate actions to improve our situation. Cognitive therapy implies when we are frightened, depressed and angry, we think and act irrationally, which leads to self-destructive behavior. Cognitive therapy requires training our minds to think rationally by controlling our thought patterns. Instead of focusing on negative thoughts, we must ask questions that will provide answers to our problems. This is a powerful tool for dealing with the negative situations we face, such as discrimination and poverty.

Never allow discrimination to destroy your dreams. We can make our world a better place if we are willing to accept the challenges life offers.

> *[T]he ideologies of racism and sexism are to a great degree inherited, they are not genetic, which is to say that just as they have been learned, they can be unlearned ... For that day when neither exists, we must all struggle.*
> —JOHNNETTA B. COLE

It is everyone's responsibility to break the cycle of discrimination. Establish new standards of learning. Accept your responsibility to retrain the morally sick who subscribe and perpetrate the horrors of discrimination in our society.

Now you should be asking yourself, How and when should I address discrimination? The answer is a simple one: Address discrimination whenever it appears. Never wait for a better opportunity to come along. If you choose to wait, you have given your permission and endorsed discrimination as a way of life.

Whenever you address discrimination, you must act with integrity, intelligence, honesty, common sense, and with the spirit of God in your heart. If you do this you will never lose; you will be filled with all the riches and rewards that life offers. You will enrich the lives of others when you work to ensure equality and equal opportunity for all. Henry Ford II explained it this way: "Our country is still young and its potential is still enormous. We should remember, as we look toward the future, that the more fully we believe in and achieve freedom and equal opportunity, not simply for ourselves but for others, the greater our accomplishments as a nation will be."

Other Important Minority Issues

Minority and female employees must develop a strong network and camaraderie with each other. This is critical to their success. One of discrimination's greatest allies is the "divide and conquer" technique. When minorities and women fail to work with each other, it is easy for those who discriminate to manipulate and control them. Qualified minorities and women are prevented from succeeding, not because minorities and women do not want to work together, but because they have been conditioned to believe it is detrimental to their success. When minorities perceive that there are only limited opportunities for them, they may feel they have to compete against each other for those few opportunities. For this reason, minorities and women are often reluctant to associate with other employees of their own race or gender, work with them or provide assistance to them. Where employment quotas exist, a minority employee is often hired to replace another minority employee. Therefore, minority employees often feel that if they help other minorities they will soon be unemployed.

Minorities often feel management frowns upon them associating with other minority employees. They feel it hurts their image and opportunities. For example, an African-American woman was hired as an administrative assistant. Her boss was an African-American male. After they had become comfortable in their working relationship, the boss confided that he had been hesitant about hiring her for fear others might think he was favoring African-American applicants. This perception is shared by most minorities and women. It is a dilemma that stifles their careers.

Too often, minority employees dislike other minorities who become successful. Jealousy and fear are major factors why minorities have difficulty working together and trusting each other. Too many minorities and women fail to support each other. The problem is not with others; it stems from within. They resent other minorities for accomplishing the things they aspire to. Minorities must control their emotions and respect the accomplishments of other minorities. They must be willing to work, support and learn from other minorities. They need to be aware that fighting each other for a small piece of the pie is useless for all concerned. Only when minorities and women work together will they be able to overcome bigoted attitudes and practices.

Minorities also need to change their own attitudes and approaches. We should challenge discriminatory behavior when we witness it or are victims of it. We should also make allowances for ignorance and insensitivity. There will be instances where acts that we perceive as discriminatory are not really based on discrimination. Find creative ways of addressing these situations. Give perpetrators a chance to resolve discriminatory problems. Here's a common scenario: You attend a meeting; everyone around the table except you is a white male. At some point during the meeting you make a suggestion. Nobody really responds. Then 15 minutes later, someone else makes virtually the same suggestion, and suddenly everyone responds with enthusiasm. This makes you wonder why your comment did not have the same impact. Was there something wrong with the way you communicated it? Or are people not taking you seriously because you are a member of a minority?

One way to deal with this type of situation would be to meet with the meeting facilitator afterwards and talk about the problem. Don't immediately make a charge of prejudice or discrimination. Instead, phrase it as a request for advice on how to make your opinions better heard — "It's strange, you know — I made the same suggestion as John, but nobody seemed to acknowledge it; can you tell me what I did wrong?" This way you are making someone in authority aware of your concerns without being confrontational. As described in the conflict resolution techniques above, you are giving them a way to correct a problem without making them look bad.

* * *

Overcoming problems and conflicts at work is an ongoing process. Each day presents new challenges. Use this formula to solve problems or conflicts you encounter.

- 80% of problem solving is identifying the problem
- 10% is defining the solution
- 10% is doing it

As simple as this formula appears, it is effective in overcoming problems and conflicts. Apply it to all your challenging situations.

Chapter 11

Rebounding After Termination

*Never let your head hang down. Never give up and sit
down and grieve. Find another way. And don't pray when
it rains if you don't pray when the sun shines.*
— SATCHEL PAIGE

To OVERCOME the adversities associated with being fired or laid
off, be willing to "fall seven times, stand up eight," as the
Japanese proverb says. Have the courage and physical and emotional stamina to face the setbacks encountered during your career.

If your employment is terminated, take immediate action to find
or create new employment for yourself. Never give up your dreams
because of the obstacles you encounter. Don't become paralyzed or
irrational due to fear or anger. If you do, it destroys your opportunities to find meaningful employment.

Experiencing a brief period of personal grief after losing a job is
normal and healthy. We must never ignore this pain and grief but
deal with them wisely. It is natural to feel angry, humiliated and
even depressed, but these conditions should only last for a short
time. It is not normal or healthy to feel angry, humiliated or
depressed for long periods. Move past these negative feelings as
quickly as possible. Use your grief and pain to empower you to find
a satisfactory career.

Find positive ways to release your anger and frustrations or they
will consume and destroy you. Sit down by yourself. Have several
healthy cries. Scream and holler at the top of your lungs. This is
often a great physical and emotional release which has a calming

effect. It is an effective outlet for releasing the anger, tensions and frustrations that build up when we are out of work without harming ourselves and others.

Seek guidance from trusted friends or knowledgeable individuals. They can provide proper direction, comfort and assistance. Listen objectively, accept honest and valuable recommendations. Acknowledge faults. Be willing to make tough decisions that empower you. It is helpful to find others who have been through your situation and successfully overcame it. They can be inspirational and helpful in your healing process.

Choose counsel wisely. Be selective in seeking advice and assistance from family and friends. Close friends and families may have your best interests at heart, but their advice may make matters worse. This does not mean do not speak with them. It means never accept unwise advice.

Never avoid family members or friends because of shame or embarrassment. Seek their comfort, advice and assistance. This is different from whining and complaining. Many individuals love to indulge their misery by constantly talking about their problems and how life is so unfair. They fail to move forward because they never learn from their experiences and the wisdom of others. They refuse to put forth the necessary effort to overcome problems, and are more interested in complaining than improving their lives.

During grieving periods never direct your frustrations or fears at yourself or innocent family members and friends. Unfortunately, this is a common occurrence. Many of us improperly displace our anger and frustrations on ourselves or the ones we love. They are convenient targets who often do not fight back. We lash out at others in the hope it will make us feel better. It is an indication we have lost control. We require professional help if we are unable to quickly eradicate this behavior.

Do not mentally torment yourself because you were fired or laid off, even if it was your fault. Instead, focus on improving your current and future situation. Don't dwell on the past, because changing it is impossible. Use the past as a teaching tool, not to punish yourself. You must overcome your emotional trauma before you can find peace and harmony. When you reach this state you'll be able to think and act objectively and improve your current difficulties. It will prevent you from taking your frustrations out on yourself and others.

The key to overcoming your grief is not to wallow in a sea of self pity. Being fired does not mean you are a failure. Robert Half, an expert in career placement, provides some insight into being fired. In his book, *How to Get a Better Job in This Crazy World,* he states that, based on surveys conducted by his organization, one out of every four of workers will be fired at some point. He is not referring to high school or college students. He is referring to competent, professional, highly skilled employees.

Empower yourself by using two steps to overcome the pain of being fired or laid off. The first is to establish a reason that turns this experience into a positive situation. Once you find a worthwhile reason, it helps you overcome feelings of depression. The second step is to decide what specific actions to take to make this experience meaningful. Millions have turned negative situations into positive experiences. Many overcame experiences that were far worse then being fired. Viktor E. Frankl's book, *Man's Search For Meaning,* shows how even the worst experiences can add value and meaning to our lives.

Frankl was a Jewish psychiatrist who survived years in Nazi concentration camps as a slave laborer. He was beaten, tortured, and was denied proper food, clothing, medical attention and sleep. His father, mother, brother and wife died in concentration camps or gas ovens. Frankl not only survived this horrible experience, he used it to improve his life and others'. He accomplished this by establishing a meaning for his suffering.

While he was in concentration camps, Frankl saw himself surviving the ordeal. He envisioned himself speaking in well-lit, warm and pleasurable lecture rooms. He would see the faces of his audience as he explained the horrors that he and others endured. He felt if he lived to tell his story he could prevent it from ever happening again. This belief gave meaning to his suffering. It gave him the will to live and overcome the degradation he experienced each day.

Viktor Frankl used this experience to mold his and others' lives when he was freed from the concentration camps. He developed a new approach to psychotherapy called "logotherapy". The basis of his theory is that the primary motivational force behind our existence is the search for meaning in our lives. Once we find meaning it gives us the strength and courage to overcome problems we encounter.

Not only can we find a meaning for our lives, we can also find meanings for specific difficult situations we encounter in life. We must take this approach if we are fired or laid off. We do this not by focusing on our present negative conditions, but by looking toward the future and the riches it has to offer. We will receive them only when we are willing to take the proper actions to improve our current situations. Viktor Frankl wrote, "The prisoner who lost faith in the future, his future was doomed. With his loss of belief in the future, he also lost his spiritual hold; he let himself decline and became subject to mental and physical decay." Many of us become prisoners of our negative thoughts when we are unemployed. We allow them to paralyze and destroy us.

We can improve ourselves only when we eliminate negative self-talk and powerless questions. They make us emotional cripples and helpless victims. When we constantly ask ourselves powerless questions such as, "Why me?" or tell ourselves "Life is so unfair," "It can't be done," or "I will never succeed," our situations become hopeless and we become victims of our circumstances. Never allow yourself to feel hopeless or victimized by circumstances. Take the advice of Anthony Davison, director of the Cornerstone Resource Development Council: "The only difference between victims and victors is how they feel about themselves." We have a choice. Feel good about yourself despite your situation. It will lead you to success. Instead of focusing on negative aspects, look for the opportunities challenges create.

Being fired does not mean we are failures. It does not mean our career is ruined or opportunities for success are lost. What we do after being fired determines if we succeed or fail. Many have experienced greater success, fame and fortunes after being fired. The opportunities to achieve these things would not have presented themselves had they never been fired. Turn the experience of being fired into a blessing in disguise as many other successful individuals have done.

Don't focus your thoughts on being fired, hurt, angry, embarrassed or guilty. Focus on what you learned from the experience and how you can apply it to improve your future. Some of the most successful men and women in the world have been fired. Many were fired more than once:

- Lee Iacocca was fired from Ford. He went on to turn Chrysler around and save it from the brink of destruction.

- Damon Wayans, popular comedian and actor who has starred in *Saturday Night Live* and *In Living Color,* and feature films, has openly and candidly discussed his experiences of being fired prior to achieving success.

- Mario Cuomo was not talented enough to play professional baseball, but he did not drown himself in self pity — he became governor of New York.

- Sally Jessy Raphael was fired more than 20 times before she became a popular talk show host.

- Thomas J. Watson became president of IBM after he was fired from National Cash Register (NCR). He was instrumental in guiding IBM from a small obscure company into one of the largest and most successful companies in the world.

As you can see from the experiences of these successful people, being fired is not the end of the world. They did not allow this unfortunate experience to prevent them from finding future success in their careers.

Success or failure is determined by the way we view our circumstances. They can liberate us or become our jailers. We become prisoners of our minds when we focus on how hopeless our circumstances are. We liberate ourselves by looking to the future and determining what we need to do today to improve it. We do this by acknowledging what is going on in our lives.

When we try to figure out why we were fired or laid off, we often find it was for one or more of the following reasons:

- Our skills deteriorated or became obsolete.
- We became too dependent on others.
- We failed to prepare for the future.
- We failed to apply ourselves.
- We did something inappropriate.
- Situation(s) happened beyond our control.

Being fired may be the catalyst to force us to take action we were too afraid to before. It is often God's way of forcing us to make a change. It can be His way of telling us to do more with our lives based on the plans He has for us.

Many employees will be terminated because they are incompetent. Unfortunately, good employees will also be terminated, laid off or forced to resign. Some reasons for terminations are fierce global competition, new technology, mergers, acquisitions, bankruptcies, relocation, plant closures, downsizing, and discrimination.

Job loss is a reality of the New Economy. It can happen to anyone at any time. Never tie your entire sense of self-worth to being employed. Employment is important and a valuable part of our lives — there is no denying this fact. However, it is also true that our purpose in life is far more than just being employed. We make important contributions to society beyond our jobs. We are teachers, leaders, mothers, fathers, and friends. There are many ways we add value to the lives of others.

Instead of allowing unemployment to cripple us, we must use it to motivate ourselves. Make an objective assessment of yourself and your situation. Be open and honest with yourself. Accept responsibility for your life and your career. During this process, identify your strengths and your weaknesses. They are equally important.

After you complete your assessment develop a well-prepared, written action plan. Take several days to complete your written action plan. This will give you time to review it and make changes.

Your written action plan must do the following:

- Identify immediate means to earn money to sustain basic household expenses (rent, food, clothing, etc.).

- Identify long-term goals and ways to achieve them (i.e., new career skills, advanced education, financial and employment security, and life style changes). Write specific plans for each area. Writing, "I am going to continue my education," is too vague. Instead, indicate a field of study, type of degree and specific goals with time frames. Indicate where you will obtain your education, how you will pay for it, and a start date.

- Divide large goals into smaller parts. List due dates for each component on a calendar to review your progress. Place it where you see it every day to review your progress and make adjustments when needed. Don't frustrate yourself by establishing unrealistic goals and time frames.

Stay focused and make a commitment to accomplish your action plan. Develop ways to keep motivated and to overcome obstacles that interfere with achieving your goals. Prepare yourself to overcome problems and setbacks.

Make the Most of Your Time

Charles Darwin said, "A man who dares to waste one hour of time has not discovered the value of life." Just because you are out of work does not mean you can sleep late or relax all day. In fact, you should wake up at your normal time or earlier. Myles Munroe explained it this way, "When you have a mission, sleep is nothing but an interruption." Looking for employment must not be considered just another chore. It must be considered your full-time occupation. View your employment search as one of your greatest investments. Read chapters 4 and 6 for effective ways or finding and creating employment for yourself.

We work eight hours a day, five days a week for others but we are not willing to devote the same time or effort for ourselves. Consider yourself as self employed. Your salary and benefits start when you find a satisfying and rewarding career. Don't limit your search to your past experience; it must include the things you love to do. Be willing to work to create the career you want.

When you are out of work, it's an excellent time to improve yourself and your skills. Enroll in courses to update your skills. There are not only college classes but a variety of educational options available — training seminars, self-improvement books, tapes and videos. Use this time to make contacts and develop good networks.

Never Fall into a Rut

Far too often we allow ourselves to fall into a rut when we are out of work. This quickly erodes our self-confidence and self-esteem. We stop taking proper care of ourselves. We began to act and look unprofessional. To prevent this from happening follow these tips:

Keep yourself neat and well groomed. Don't allow your appearance to deteriorate. Even when you have nowhere to go make sure you maintain a professional appearance. This has a very positive psychological effect. It also sends a positive message to others. It tells them you are a winner.

Don't watch TV all day. Many individuals become addicted to TV when they are unemployed. If you spend your days watching soap operas and reruns you are wasting valuable time. Use this time to develop your new career or explore employment leads.

Don't get bored. Boredom leads to depression. Depression leads to more serious problems than unemployment. Plan each day's activities in advance. Do not leave the success of your day to chance.

Never use unemployment as an excuse to develop bad habits. Bad habits limit your potential and are difficult to break. If you don't smoke, don't start. Don't start drinking excessively. Don't use illegal or harmful legal drugs to mask any pain or guilt you are experiencing. Address the root of the problem, not the side effects.

Seek professional help if you are having problems with depression, or are feeling a loss of confidence and self esteem. Seek family counseling if your family is affected. Sometimes we become so overwhelmed by our problems we need professional help to resolve them. There is nothing to be ashamed of. We all need help sometimes. If you are unable to pay for these services there many non-profit organizations that will help you for free. Most churches offer free counseling services or can refer you to them. Seek God, He will provide you with the solutions and answers to your problems.

Join in recreational activities; they allow you to relax and recharge your internal batteries. Find affordable ways to enjoy yourself. Now is your chance to spend quality time with your spouse or someone special in your life. This can be as simple as going for walks on the beach.

Develop an exercise program for yourself and stick with it. It will help you develop both the physical and mental stamina that you need to successfully find the career you seek. Exercise also helps eliminate depression by producing endorphins, brain chemicals with pain killing and tranquilizing abilities. They are what make us feel a natural high after exercising.

Develop a positive mental attitude. You will need this to sustain you through the setbacks you will encounter.

Address Your Immediate Needs

Few of us are independently wealthy, so we must find ways to support ourselves while seeking new employment. This is difficult for many of us because from early childhood we are conditioned to become employees, not employers. We're trained to be good workers — to follow directions, to conform, to dampen our creativity and curiosity. As a result, few of us ever take the time to consider or take advantage of the many financial opportunities available beyond working for someone else.

Earlier, I briefly discussed the option of self employment. When we are unemployed, it may become a matter of necessity rather than choice to start our own business. When thinking of starting a business, you must not only consider your skills, expertise and experiences but also personal interests, dreams, and hobbies. Combine this with serving the needs of others and you will find success.

It is inappropriate for others to decide what you should do. Only you can decide what is right for you. You may already know what you want to do but just never decided to do it. If you have no idea what you can or want to do now is the time to find out. Often it takes time and several failures before you find a full- or part-time business that's right for you. Don't become discouraged or give up during this exploratory stage.

There are many sources of information that can help you successfully start your new business. See the Resource section for useful books, magazines and Web sites.

Do not expect new enterprises to be successful and profitable overnight. Don't allow setbacks to discourage you or force you to give up. Consider starting more than one business to determine what is right for you. It is natural that you will face difficulties and make errors. Use them as learning tools. Even if your business does not turn out as expected, you will no doubt have increased your knowledge and skills, which will be of value to your next employer.

* * *

Being unemployed is not a crime, nor does it mean you are a failure. View it as an opportunity for personal growth. Use it to expand your horizons and discover new opportunities to express your ideas, passions, and creative talents. Now is the time to become the person you always wanted to be. Move forward in your new life with enthusiasm and confidence.

Chapter 12

Changing
Employers or Careers

We emphasize that we believe in change because we were born of it, we have lived by it, we prosper and grew great by it. So the status quo has never been our god, and we ask no one else to bow down before it.

— CARL T. ROWAN

KNOWING when and how to change employers or careers is essential to our professional growth. In chapter 10 we discussed many methods and techniques to help overcome obstacles. We explained why we must stay focused to move forward. Only by staying focused can we accomplish our goals. When we encounter circumstances that prevent our skills and abilities from being used, we enter a stage of regression and deterioration. When careers or employers create environments that are detrimental, we must consider making changes that will empower us.

We must take care before deciding to seek employment elsewhere or change careers. Our decision must be based on legitimate reasons that are in our best interest. They must not be based on emotions, revenge, or our lack of abilities.

Let's review the valid reasons for changing employment and careers:

Health Considerations

Good health ranks as one of the greatest assets we possess. Without good health we restrict the quality of our life and reduce our life span. When we consider good health, we must include physical, spiritual and mental health. Each of them are important to our success. We do not have good health if we have a healthy physical body but are experiencing emotional turmoil in our careers. This will eventually lead to the deterioration of our physical body.

Too often we jeopardize our lives by working in unsafe and unhealthy conditions because the pay is good. But if this causes our health to fail, no amount of money is worth it.

Employees have the right to work in a safe working environment. Unfortunately many companies allow working conditions that are unsafe and dangerous. Never accept unsafe working conditions. Prevent yourself from becoming a statistic. Work with employers to eliminate unsafe conditions. Many problems can be corrected with little expense. If safety hazards are costly to fix, employers must consider the potential legal liabilities they could incur.

You may be worried about losing your job if you try to address safety concerns, but consider this: Losing your position is better than losing your life. You can always find another position but you cannot find another life. If your employer is unwilling to correct unsafe conditions, report them to the proper agencies. The life you save may be your own. If unsafe conditions cannot be eliminated, find other employment.

Limited Opportunities

When we stop learning or applying ourselves we stop growing intellectually, spiritually, and professionally. The longer this condition continues the greater the damage to our careers.

To find success you must seek positions that allow you the opportunity to use your abilities and grow. Napoleon Bonaparte said it well when he said, "Ability is of little account without opportunity."

I explained in chapters 7 and 8 that you must accept the responsibility to recognize and create opportunities to achieve success in your career. There are no exceptions to this rule. If you realize that you would be more productive if you applied your efforts elsewhere, or find you are expending most of your time and energy overcoming unnecessary obstacles, it may be time to change employers.

Make changes that will enhance your position and improve opportunities for success. Be careful about making decisions; be certain you are not the cause of your problems. Review all the facts and options available. When opportunities are restricted, seek employment elsewhere.

No Career Future

New technology and ideas are constantly changing our work force. Many positions available today were unheard of 10 years ago. Positions that once were in great demand no longer exist. At one time new technology only put unskilled employees out of work. This is no longer true. It is now common for skilled laborers to be displaced by new technology and new demands. Often college graduates and seasoned professionals are displaced because they failed to update their skills or keep abreast of new developments.

This not only happens to employees but to many companies as well. They have not kept up with changes in technology, market demands, competition and society. These companies were profitable in the past but can no longer survive in today's markets. Their methods are obsolete. Their goods and services are no longer in demand.

This is not just happening to small, mom-and-pop operations that may lack the resources to keep up with new technology and market changes. In early 1999, one of America's great, successful companies, Levi-Strauss, announced it would be closing many of its North American factories and moving the jobs to lower-cost plants abroad. Most analysts have attributed the company's recent troubles to its failure to keep up with marketing trends of the '90s.

New technology is changing the way we do business, work and live. In an article in *US News and World Report*, "1996 Career Guide Cyberjobs: Technology Spells Opportunity" (October 30, 1995), almost half of the 20 hottest careers for the future were related to the computer revolution. Most new positions are created by new technology or are dependent on it.

Jobs are also being eliminated or dramatically changed by new technology. This is a horrifying prospect for unprepared employees who find their positions no longer exist or they lack the skills needed to perform their job. Everyone can face this horrible experience, regardless of how much their skills are in demand today.

The positive side of this dilemma is that we can avoid it by planning for the future. We must accept that change is inevitable. We must prepare ourselves for this challenge. Occupations and skills do not become obsolete overnight. There are early signs that occupations are going to undergo changes. But often we choose to ignore them until it is too late.

Instead, we spend our energy fighting against change or ignoring it. We live in the present and fail to prepare for the future. We allow our fear of change to paralyze us. It is our responsibility to be aware of what is going on in our chosen field. We can't rely on employers to protect us; companies can fall prey to the same assumptions and fears about the future that individuals do.

Do not wait until the bottom falls out of your industry, your employer closes operations, or you receive a termination notice to change careers or upgrade your skills. Prepare for employment or career changes before being forced to leave. Develop new skills so you can leave on your terms before disaster strikes. Be prepared to find employment or new careers in another industry or with employers that have a future. Consider school or home study courses to upgrade or acquire new skills. If your skills are obsolete, be willing to accept lower positions to acquire the training, skills and experience you need.

Never ignore changing employment markets. If you do, you will find no future in your career and never achieve success. Be prepared and willing to make changes in your career or employer when it is in your best interest. Do this before your career or company becomes obsolete and you become an unemployment statistic.

Financial Compensation

Employees should always receive fair compensation for their efforts, skills and abilities. Our level of pay is an indicator of how much our employer values us and our work.

When reviewing the salary issue, remember there are other forms of compensation to consider, such as the opportunity to obtain important skills and experiences that increase our future earning potential. Security is another important factor that must not be overlooked.

As our skills and performance increase, so should our level of pay. There are wide ranges of salaries between different employees and employers. Know what other employees with similar levels of experience and skills are paid, both within and outside your company. You may find great disparities in salaries. Employees often exaggerate their salaries, so verify them when possible.

If you find you are making significantly less than others in comparable positions, review your options for improving your financial position. Many employees are underpaid and are not aware of their worth and potential earning capacity.

If you are underpaid, consider speaking with your superiors. Know how much you want. Your salary request must be reasonable. Be prepared for objections. Be ready to show your value to your employer. Don't ask for a raise if you are a marginal employee. Nothing aggravates supervisors more than employees who make little difference to the firm asking for raises. These employees are likely to find themselves out of work.

Never approach supervisors with ultimatums. Never make threats such as if you do not receive a raise, you will look for another position. This is the fastest way to create bad feelings and find yourself unemployed. Instead, make an appointment for a performance review. Be ready to show your contributions to the firm; give examples of how you've saved money or brought in new sources of income. Provide salary comparisons to others in your field.

Be prepared for common answers used to justify not giving employees raises, such as they are only allowed to give performance raises once a year. If this is the kind of response you receive, try four methods to overcome their objections:

- Ask for a salary adjustment. Salary adjustments are increases in pay to compensate employees who are underpaid. Negotiate with your employer to receive it immediately, not when annual raises are given.
- If your supervisor insists they can't justify giving you a raise or salary adjustment, ask for a promotion. Be prepared to show that you are ready for additional responsibilities.
- If no position is available, ask them to create one for you by giving you a new title and additional duties. If this isn't feasible, ask to be considered for the next available position. Ask the supervisor to set a time frame for this.
- If these requests fail, ask for a bonus. Bonuses are often given to employees who perform at high standards.

If your company is not agreeable to any of these recommendations, it is time to review your options. Consider advancement, salary opportunities, benefits and job security. Compare your skills and abilities to other individuals and their salaries. Estimate what your salary will be 10 years from now based on the present salary guidelines and promotional opportunities. Determine what is the highest position you could obtain and what would be the lowest position you would accept. You may find out that you would be disappointed. Your only option may be to seek greater financial rewards elsewhere.

Lack of Personal Fulfillment

We spend more than one third of our lives at work. If our work gives us little satisfaction, it creates a void in our lives that can make us feel worthless and unfulfilled. It is impossible for this empty feeling not to spill over into our personal lives. It is sheer torture to go to a job we dislike every day. It places a tremendous strain on our physical and emotional health. Sooner or later our drive and performance suffers. We lose confidence in ourselves. We fall into a rut, and start feeling depressed and in poor health.

Finding work that provides personal satisfaction is more important than filling our bank accounts. If we love our careers, we will be successful. "No person who is enthusiastic about his work has anything to fear from life," said Samuel Godwyn. We will never find success or happiness if we choose professions that are unsatisfying to us.

It is common for employees to remain in the same position year after year and never find personal satisfaction or happiness. Other dissatisfied employees will change jobs but not careers. Each new job is more disappointing than the previous one. They select these jobs based on their known skills and experience. They fail to select new careers based on their interests. People who do not know what professions they would enjoy fail to take the necessary steps to discover them. They are unwilling to experiment with different occupations or to take a chance to find a career that would be satisfying to them. Their fears overpower their interest and enthusiasm to try something different.

Ralph Waldo Emerson wrote, "Every great and commanding movement in the annals of the world is the triumph of enthusiasm. Nothing great was ever achieved without it." Find work that you are enthusiastic about and you will find success in all your endeavors. If this requires you to change employment or careers, so be it. Do this expediently with all your zest, abilities, and skills. With your new-found enthusiasm you will discover success and fulfillment in your work.

Discrimination

In some situations where we encounter discrimination, it is not in our best interest to spend all our time and energy directly confronting it. This does not mean we should ignore discrimination; it means we must carefully choose the appropriate time and place to make our stand.

It is impossible to change beliefs of someone who refuses to change. Trying to do so often leads to greater animosity. Instead of a direct frontal assault, consider other, more productive strategies. Find ways to make the most of these situations. Use them as learning experiences to help you accomplish your goals.

It is usually a losing battle for a small army to directly attack a larger army that has superior fire power. Large and small corporations and companies have superior firepower in the form of lawyers and laws that are in their favor. They also have financial resources and the time to wear you down.

On the other hand, many smaller armies have been successful in defeating larger adversaries by using tactics and strategies that give them the advantage. They capitalized on their opponent's ignorance. They used their adversary's unsound practices against them. Instead of playing to their strengths they capitalized on their weakness. They cut off the supplies they need to keep alive (food, water, ammunition). This causes opponents to weaken and seek negotiations.

We can take this approach in dealing with discriminatory companies. We can cut into their customer base by establishing our own businesses, creating new markets, and hiring the most talented people available. Instead of being employees we can become employers.

We must not rely on others for our success. We have to become self sufficient. We must serve as leaders and examples to other minorities and women to show them we can succeed in spite of prejudice directed toward us. For instance, blacks spend 267 billion dollars a year in disposable income and spend less than 10 per cent of that in the black community. The time, money and energy we spend trying to make companies stop discriminating could be used to start our own successful businesses in our own communities. In doing so we'll be able to use all our abilities and talents. We will only be restricted by the limitations we place on ourselves. In some cases, this may be a more effective way of showing the futility of discrimination. A company or organization that fails to support and encourage minority and women employees not only loses valuable employees but is also cutting itself off from profitable markets.

Consider the person you will become if you confront discrimination at your place of employment. Will it make you resentful, unhappy and lose focus on the things you want to accomplish? Will it negatively affect your physical and emotional health? Will it affect you in other ways? If it will, carefully consider other options that will enhance your situation, not hinder it. This does not mean you are quitting; it means you are using a different, more effective approach.

There can be negative repercussions in not taking direct action to deal with discrimination and racism. Consider how it will affect you if don't do something to correct this situation. Will it hinder your future plans or place your present position in danger? There are situations when it is your duty to directly confront discrimination swiftly and vigorously.

Your decision to directly or indirectly address discrimination must depend on determining the most effective way to eradicate discrimination and enhance your position. Carefully review the facts. Base your decision on past, current and future considerations. Never base your decision on emotions alone. Be objective; respond to discrimination in a way that will improve your situation and that of others.

Never Allow Fear to Control You

Never allow fear to prevent you from changing careers. Often we are trained in one field but discover it does not give us the fulfillment we seek. We discover other interests and professions that give the satisfaction we miss in our current profession. When exploring employment options, don't always think in terms of what you have done in the past; think of what you would *like* to do. This type of thinking provides unlimited possibilities.

There are valid and invalid reasons for changing careers. Change should only occur after careful consideration. It should not be an impulsive decision. Nor should we continue in a profession for foolish reasons. Staying in a profession to prove a point or to please or hurt others is a waste of your life.

We should not change careers because we think others are the source of our unhappiness. Each individual must accept responsibility for his or her happiness. Happiness must be created within ourselves. If we are unhappy with our profession, we must be willing to change it.

The Correct Way to Leave

Let's review the rules for leaving employers. As previously discussed in chapter 3, it is easier to obtain new employment when we are already employed. If you are leaving of your own accord, find another position before you resign.

Being employed makes it easier to find employment. Being employed carries prestige. It is unfair, but being unemployed raises questions about your character. The first question interviewers will ask is, "Why are you unemployed?" Next they will wonder whether you did something wrong, if you were fired, how you are supporting yourself, and whether you are desperate for work. Waiting until you are out of work to seek a new employer puts you in an unpromising position.

If you are going to leave your employer, prepare for your departure. Try to leave on good terms and resolve any existing problems prior to leaving. Don't create new problems because you plan to leave. Maintain a professional standard of work. Be selective when informing others you are looking for a new position. If you are not careful, it will quickly become front-page news at your office.

Remember, good references are essential to finding employment. You will need references from your current and previous employers. Know what references you will receive from them. Never assume that everyone will give you a great reference. First, obtain their permission. Next, find out how they will rate you. Do they consider you an excellent, good, fair or unsatisfactory employee? Would they rehire you?

Select employers and supervisors who will give you good references. You do not want to use anyone who will give you a negative reference. Find out what they see as your strong and weak points. Most potential employers are skeptical of references that show employees as perfect. Everyone has weaknesses. Employers will accept employees with minor weakness.

When interviewing, use references from former employers and associates. Employers understand you cannot use your current employer as a reference until after they offer you a position. Employment offers are often contingent on a good reference from your present employer.

When you leave an employer, try to obtain written references. This is important because many employers promise they will give you an excellent reference but have no intention of doing so. In other cases your references may move on and you'll have no way of contacting them. Try to obtain their home address and phone numbers so you can keep in touch with them. Do not ask for a written reference from current employers until after you've given notice or unless you know it will not jeopardize your job.

The best references are from people whom you've worked for. They are familiar with your work. Their references are far better than those from employees in Human Resources, who usually don't know you or your work. HR people tend to provide generic references, which are not very impressive. It is always best to obtain written and verbal references from employees with important titles, such as managers, controllers, vice presidents and presidents, who are familiar with your work.

Whenever you obtain a letter of recommendation, you want one that enhances your chances for a new position. It should show your accomplishments, how and why you were an asset to the company, and why they would rehire you.

If you are leaving your place of employment and are negotiating the terms of your severance package, make sure you include a good written reference as a component. It is important that you review and agree upon the written reference prior to leaving or signing any agreements. Make sure you receive a copy of it.

If possible, never quit your position before you obtain new employment. When you are employed, it provides valuable leverage and more options. It prevents you from accepting positions out of desperation. It allows you the time to find what types of positions and careers are available. It gives you the luxury to carefully shop around for the best position. Being employed eliminates stress and discomfort when looking for new employment.

Final Considerations

Do not allow biased thinking to distort your judgment when changing employers or careers. Carefully review your entire situation, not small, fragmented segments of what's going on. Make sure you are changing for the right reasons. Use the following guidelines to help you when making employment or career changes.

- Only make changes when it allows you the opportunity to move forward. Moving forward must not be considered only in terms of monetary gains. It must include values, spiritual growth and the level of contributions to family and our society.

- Do not allow invalid excuses, such as family or financial obligations, to prevent you from changing. Because of your love for your family, you have a duty to seek the best possible life for them. Do not dishonor yourself and your family by blaming them for your refusal to take action. Financial problems usually arise because you have not allowed yourself the opportunity to grow and improve your present situation. There are greater risks in playing it safe when it prevents us from using opportunities that will enhance our lives.

- When opportunities are not equally available to all parties and our personal growth is impeded, it is time to move on. If our employer does not value us and our abilities are overlooked, when we are repeatedly and unfairly passed over after paying our dues, when others of lesser or equal talent are given opportunities to move forward — we must move on.

- When our ideas and work are ignored or not recognized sufficiently, or if others are always permitted to reap the rewards of our labor, we must examine other options. If this situation happens once or twice it may not be reason for concern. It is called "paying our dues." We must show we can handle responsibility and pressure and can generate the desired results. It's a different situation if our ideas or work is of such a magnitude it deserves recognition and the appropriate rewards are never received.

- Before you leave your employer, carefully consider every option possible. Are there other departments or other individuals you can work for within the organization? Can they give you opportunities, challenges and growth? Consider transferring to other departments or locations before leaving your present company.

- Understand that making a change will not eliminate problems. In fact, we incur more problems when we make significant changes. We change not to avoid problems, but due to a lack of opportunities and challenges. We make the most of our lives when we face and overcome problems.

- Do not let your ego prevent you from changing when it is in your best interest. Only by acknowledging your mistakes can you begin to make changes to improve your life. If you've selected a wrong career, one that gives you little or no purpose or fulfillment, admit it and move on.

- Do not think you failed or are a quitter if you cannot make a situation work for you. Most of us were taught to never quit. We need to change the phrase from "never quit" to "never quit trying to improve our lives." This gives us power and flexibility. We learn by acknowledging mistakes and making changes when it is in our best interest. Never feel you failed or gave up if you make a change that improves your life.

Knowing when and when not to change careers or employers is essential to our personal, professional, spiritual, and financial growth. Make changes that empower you and allow you to move forward. Change for the sake of change is of little value when it fails to add something to our lives. Change is necessary when we stop growing. Change is the road that allows us to reach our purpose in life. If we achieve our purpose in life, change allows us to maintain our level of success.

As important as making changes is never compromising our core principles and beliefs to achieve our goals. The only exceptions are when experience, personal growth, and spiritual and moral evolution show our core beliefs were wrong. Our core principles and beliefs are the essence of what we are and what we will become.

Chapter 13

Maintaining Success

Life affords no higher pleasure than that of surmounting difficulties, passing from one step of success to another, forming new wishes and seeing them gratified.
—SAMUEL JOHNSON

EVERYONE achieves some level of success. The problem lies in maintaining and improving upon it. Never allow success to mislead you. Do not let success make you feel superior to others. Never allow vain thoughts or flattery to inflate your ego. "Sweet praise is like perfume, it is fine if you don't swallow it," as Dwight D. Eisenhower wisely put it.

Never believe you are infallible because of prior successes. Continue to do the things that created your success. Believing that once you achieve success you will live a carefree life is foolish. Maintaining success places us in a position of responsibility. Not only must we use the abilities that created our success, we have to continually add new skills to our repertoire.

Strangely, many successful individuals find the price of success too high. They find it so overwhelming they choose to sabotage their success. How can this be, when so many of us seek success? Most of us are only prepared to handle the positive aspects of success. We are unprepared to face the difficulties that come with it. Success can become a tremendous burden if we are not equipped to handle the responsibilities it brings.

Success can be a disappointment if we do not master the skills necessary to make it challenging, rewarding, and enjoyable. When we apply success skills, they remove the burdens associated with the process of succeeding. Success skills turn unbearable situations into interesting and intriguing challenges. Only when we master success skills will we cherish success and be unwilling to give it up for any price.

Become a Leader

Becoming successful without leadership qualities is not impossible, but it would be extremely difficult and frustrating. Leaders possess the ability to solicit and recruit the assistance of others. This decreases the time and effort a single individual needs to put forth. The ability to lead enables a single individual to take on massive projects that are impossible to complete alone. Most goals in life are impossible to accomplish without the contributions of others.

Leadership is a skill that must be cultivated. It can be developed and mastered by anyone. Too many of us falsely believe leadership is a quality that some of us are born with. It is true that many individuals display exceptional leadership abilities from an early age with little training. They are simply using leadership skills which allow them to think and act like leaders. These skills can be learned.

Before we can lead others, we must possess the ability to lead ourselves. It requires four steps to accomplish this:

1. Establish worthwhile goals.
2. Develop detailed plans to accomplish your goals.
3. Take the necessary actions to achieve your goals.
4. Develop the discipline and fortitude to accomplish your goals.

Ineffective leaders rely on force, fear or guilt as their primary means to solicit the assistance of others. If you use these methods to obtain the help of others, you diminish your co-workers', team's or subordinates' performance. Never assume that becoming a manager automatically makes you a leader. Exceptional leaders understand that "leadership [is] the art of getting someone else to do something you want done because he wants to do it" (Dwight D. Eisenhower). Exceptional leaders possess the ability to persuade others to willingly help them accomplish their goals.

Be a Good Judge of Character

Place individuals in positions or levels of responsibility that match their abilities and character. We often make the mistake of hiring the wrong employee for a position. We hire employees who meet the educational and work experience requirements but lack the character needed to do the job. These individuals do not possess the ethical or moral character to perform at their best.

Being qualified means we not only possess the necessary academic background and experience, but also the moral conviction to perform to the best of our abilities. There are too many educated employees who obtain advanced degrees for the wrong reasons. Their sole purpose is to gain prestige and money so they do not have to work hard. They believe their duty is to make everyone else work. They contribute little or nothing to their employers.

Become an Objective Thinker

Develop clarity of thinking. Without clarity of thought we can never rely on ourselves to develop solutions to difficult problems. Wise decisions are not based on subjective or biased opinions.

This is a dilemma. Most individuals believe they are objective thinkers when they are not. One way to learn if you are objective is to see yourself from your opponent's point of view. You may discover the way you think and act is subjective and not in your best interest. Ask yourself if you would understand or respect your decisions and actions if you were on the receiving end of them. Even if you didn't agree, would you understand that there are valid reasons for these actions?

Objective thinkers fully understand and foresee the impact of their actions. They are prepared to address the issues fairly. They are open to suggestions and recommendations. Objective thinkers are willing to change opinions. They never allow their egos to prevent them from correcting bad decisions or accepting the ideas and opinions of others.

To be objective we must possess the ability to make wise decisions. Knowledge alone is not sufficient to make the right choice or ensure our success. It must be combined with the magic of wisdom to make it effective. Wisdom is the ability to effectively use our knowledge and experiences to make good decisions based on the facts available. This explains why even geniuses can be unsuccessful. They may lack the wisdom to use their abilities to enhance their position.

Wisdom is more powerful than the greatest armies. When we combine knowledge and wisdom, they lead to the right decisions.

Responsibility Must Be Accompanied by Authority

Many successful and talented individuals fail not because they lack abilities or didn't make the necessary effort, but because they were never provided with the authority equivalent to their responsibility.

The simple fact that managers have authority over subordinates provides an important advantage even if it is never used. Employees are willing to listen to supervisors who have the authority to affect their careers. Subordinates and peers respond differently to supervisors who have authority than they do to those who don't. Subordinates respect authority even when it is not used. Responsibility without authority guarantees failure. If supervisors do not have the authority to act against employees who fail to perform, it undermines their position.

If you lack the authority that should come with a supervisory position, succeeding is impossible. Individuals in positions of responsibility must have the authority to take disciplinary action, give promotions, change policies and procedures, negotiate agreements, and make recommendations. Whenever you are offered a position make sure you are given the authority to go with it. Be clear on your level of authority before you accept a new position.

We Must Not Only Prepare for the Future, We Must Embrace It

Our success is determined by how well we prepare for the future. Too often we believe that preparing for the future means waiting for a change to take place and then being a part of it. If we react to change after it has taken place we miss important opportunities. We find ourselves in the role of playing catch-up.

Following the leader makes you a follower. Some of the largest and most successful companies and individuals are discovering a frightening truth. The ideas that were their key to success are now leading them to disaster. In the past, prior to making major changes, these companies took years scrutinizing, studying and evaluating. This was the normal cycle for companies. Today this luxury is no longer available. With national and global competition, whoever reacts first becomes the leader. They achieve success because they seize the small window of opportunity.

To be successful we must place ourselves into positions where we have the flexibility to change and the insight to recognize opportunities. Successful companies create new interests in old goods or services. They can create new products, ideas and services. They must recognize new trends and developments in their early stage.

The ability to react in a timely fashion is the key to success. You cannot react quickly if you are unaware of what's going on. Stay abreast of developments and trends. Keep in touch not only with your field but with what's happening beyond it. Exchange ideas with people outside your industry as well as with fellow employees.

We gain valuable insight by expanding our circle of acquaintances. Do not limit the exchange of ideas to executives, professionals or people of power. Be open to everyone's ideas, whatever their position or stature. Everyone has valuable sources of information.

Develop a reading program that includes newspapers, books and magazines. Read technical books and magazines that pertain to your field. Read about the latest developments in technology, future trends, science, finance, and social issues. Make reading and studying the future a daily habit.

Take courses and attend meetings of professional organizations. Use the latest developments and technology to enhance your performance. Do not focus on the present; look toward the future. We can no longer limit our concerns to the small domains of our personal and professional lives. We must be aware of what is happening outside our neighborhoods and cities. We must concern ourselves with changes made on national and international levels. Today whatever happens in other cities, states and countries affects our lives. We must prepare for these changes and their impact. Use this information to improve your life.

In her book, *The Popcorn Report,* Faith Popcorn states, "The future is serious business and if your customers reach the future before you, they'll leave you behind." The things that made us successful yesterday may bring us failure in future. The future has redefined the way we think, act and relate to others. The old rules no longer apply. New opportunities not only enhance our lives but the world as we know it.

In the past, current information meant data that were months or years old. This is no longer the case. Now we need up-to-the-minute information. In the book *Information Anxiety,* author R. S. Wurman explains that the amount of information available to us doubles every five years. We are constantly seeking better methods to access and use this information productively. If we do not have the ability or knowledge to use this information we cannot be successful. Up-to-date information provides an edge and helps us to successfully compete.

The rapidity of change is evident in the new terminology created daily to describe technological developments. We now use terminology and acronyms such as e-commerce, virtual corporations, discontinuity trend analysis, cyberspace, ISP, HTML and gigbytes — just to name a few. How many of these terms do you recognize? Can you explain what they mean? Can you explain how they will have an impact on your life? If you don't know what they mean, can you find this information? You will find these terms used in current articles, magazines and books describing developments in various fields. These and other terms have a major impact on our lives. You cannot properly plan or react to changes if you have no idea what's going on. You must be well informed and knowledgeable to recognize and take advantage of opportunities.

Not all trends should be followed or subscribed to. Some are flash trends — they end faster than they start. Worthwhile trends are best used when they are first taking off or at the middle of their peak. If you get involved in a trend in its infancy, it may place you as a leader in the industry. The Internet is a good example. Companies like Yahoo got in on the Internet trend before most of the general public had heard of it. They correctly anticipated that the Internet would be more than a fad. They invested time and money to establish a foothold on the information highway. Today Yahoo has one of the most popular search engines on the Internet and has experienced spectacular, unprecedented growth.

Trends are not just fads. They are the starting points for new technology, industries, skills, goods and services. They affect our quality of life. They can make what we do obsolete or make our future secure. In the future new trends and technology will eliminate many careers, but there is a positive flipside to this evolution process. For every position or career eliminated, three to four new careers or employment opportunities are created. The problem is that most people are unwilling to retrain for them. Identify new business and employment opportunities and trends. Prepare for them by retraining and developing the skills to exploit these opportunities.

Make Education a Lifelong Occupation

We must continue our education to be successful. This may require going to college, trade or technical schools. Many excuses used in the past for not continuing our education are no longer valid. They include, "Schools are too expensive." "I can't get to school." "There are no schools nearby." "I don't have the time." "I work erratic hours." "I get home too late." "I don't have a babysitter." In other chapters, I've discussed how on-line services and the Internet can help us find employment, do research, and circulate our resumés. Now we can also use the technology to upgrade our education.

Technology provides a convenient way to continue our education with distance education. The term "distance education" simply refers to learning that is delivered by technology — cable television, satellite transmission, video and audio tape, voice mail, fax and computers (E-mail, Web sites, electronic bulletin boards, video conferencing). You learn outside the traditional classroom setting — at a distance — whether you're a few miles or half a world away. Classes can be recorded and watched at your convenience. Using this technology, Great Britain's Open University has attracted more than 150,000 students worldwide. More than 75 reputable American colleges and universities offer undergraduate and Master degree distance programs. Over four million Americans are using their computers to obtain professional credentials at less than half the cost of traditional schools.

Be aware that not all distance or home study courses are reputable. Unaccredited school curriculums range from poor to excellent. To find which schools offer the best on-line or cable programs and curriculums, contact the Distance Education and Training Council. They accredit home study programs offered in the USA and can recommend excellent distance education programs.

Show Appreciation to Others

Always show your appreciation toward others who help and support you. Never take others for granted or take advantage of their thoughtfulness. Rewarding people with monetary compensation is not always the most effective way of showing gratitude. Take the time to personally thank individuals who helped you directly or indirectly. A friendly smile and warm thank-you go a long way in showing your appreciation. If you are unable to personally thank someone, call them or send a thank-you card or other appropriate token of appreciation. Be willing to reward their kindness by supporting them in their actions when it is appropriate.

Show your appreciation by giving others credit and recognition for their work or assistance. Be consistent and fair when rewarding employees, colleagues and business associates. Make sure it is appropriate; if it is not, others may misunderstand and resent your actions.

Do not make the mistake of feeling obligated to repay kindness or support by placing yourself in a compromising position. If someone helps you only to make you feel obligated to help them, they are not friends. This must be considered a business arrangement and treated as such. Neither party should intentionally place the other party in a compromising position by making them feel obligated.

A Positive Image

The image we project is our most important asset. We are not just judged by how much we know or how well we perform. We are judged based on what others think of us — our image.

This image is determined by the way we present ourselves and communicate with others. As indicated in chapter 5, communication is determined by verbal and non-verbal messages. It includes not only what we say but also our manner of speech, tone of voice, timing, pauses, and how well we connect with others. This in turn includes appearance, body language, actions, and our reactions to others. How well we create rapport with others determines it. Remember, the verbal or non-verbal messages we want to convey are often not the messages received by our audience. Make sure the message your audience receives is the message you meant to send.

At work and social functions, avoid sexist, racial or political remarks whenever possible. Don't make insensitive comments. Be sensitive and considerate of delicate situations. Control your emotions when you are upset. Think before you speak or act. Keep in touch with changing attitudes, laws and behavior. What is accepted today can become taboo tomorrow. Avoid excessive alcohol, gossip, dancing, opinions, etc., at these events. The way you conduct yourself at social functions will not be forgotten. It will be taken into account during reviews, merit increases and potential advancement opportunities. Office parties or other social functions are not the place to let your hair down and make a fool of yourself. It is professional suicide and will restrict or end your career. Never make the mistake of trying emulate your boss or other high-level management at social functions. Management makes allowances and overlooks indiscretions of upper management while they hold lower-level employees accountable.

Show concern for others' ideas and opinions. Listen to what others have to say before you make a decision. Admit when you are wrong. Make apologies without being asked and accept them when they are offered.

You Can't Please Everyone So Don't Try

Understand you cannot please everyone. Regardless of what you do or say, there will always be someone who will not be satisfied. In fact, trying to please everyone is not a worthwhile goal. Instead establish a goal to treat people fairly when completing your objectives. Be prepared to handle criticism or rejection by others who do not agree with you.

Hire Qualified Employees

You are only as good as the people who work for you. Your successes or failures are a direct indication of the competency of your subordinates. It is easy for one individual to spoil your reputation or the reputation of your organization. It is also true that one individual can elevate you and your company. This is why hiring the best employees available is important.

The best employees are not always the ones with the most degrees, best work experience or highest salaries. Performance is determined by attitude, skills and the ability to use them. I had the experience of hiring an employee without a degree and with little experience for an important position. She became the most impressive employee I ever hired. Initially I was not considering this person for the position but after speaking with her, I changed my mind. This individual was honest and forthright in acknowledging she lacked important qualifications and experience needed for this position. What she lacked in formal education and experience, she made up for in other qualities. She showed she was honest and trustworthy. She had a strong desire to succeed and learn.

This employee was determined and did not give up when I said she was not qualified. She replied that she had never been given the chance to show what she could accomplish. She confidently asked for the opportunity to help me accomplish my goals. She not only explained how she would perform her duties, but also made recommendations to improve the department.

During our interview, this applicant made me realize she was special, capable and willing to do whatever it took to perform satisfactorily. I hired this employee even though she lacked experience. I never had any regrets. Her work was exceptional. She performed beyond my wildest imagination. In a short period she corrected all major problems. She turned out to be one of my best employees.

Planning and Organization

Having the finest education or skills or a brilliant mind means nothing if you are unable to make your ideas a reality. To transform your ideas into reality requires planning, organization and the skills to take your ideas from conception to completion.

The ability to organize and properly plan your activities is a powerful skill. Organization protects our greatest asset — our time.

Being organized and well prepared does not mean becoming a fanatic and planning everything down to the last minute or second. It means planning your days to make the time to accomplish your goals. Incorporate the helpful tips below into your daily lifestyle. They will help you control your time and accomplish important goals.

Establish written short- and long-term goals with completion dates. We should review important goals daily. Each night review your day's progress. Indicate what you completed. Prepare a written list of what you want to accomplish the next day. Use this list as your guide.

Use an appointment book. This is a valuable tool for managing your time and staying on top of your work.

Plan for success by taking immediate action. Too many of us are waiting for something magical to happen that will instantly make us motivated or successful. If you wait for motivation or success, it will never happen.

Organize work areas a minimum of two times a day. Our work area is a reflection on us. An untidy work area is an indication of sloppy work habits and performance. Organize papers and files so you can quickly find information. File papers by date, alphabetically or numerically. File like items together. Use labels, folders and file cabinets. File information after using it.

Don't be a pack rat but do not discard information you need. Learn to properly purge files and use long-term storage facilities.

If you are unable to accomplish your goals you have failed to properly plan and organize your time. Your time is the most valuable asset you have. Know the difference between using your time productively and wasting it. Example: You should not expend the same time and effort to resolve a $10,000,000 problem as you would a $35 problem.

Treat Each Person as an Individual

Never get caught up in the belief that everyone should be treated the same. It is neither realistic nor conducive to good business. It is more realistic to treat each person fairly and respectfully. Beware of individuals who proclaim they treat all people the same. This cliché is often used by employers in referring to how they treat minorities and women. Minorities and women do not want to be treated the same as others. They want to be treated fairly and as individuals. Each individual should be judged and treated according to their performance and contributions.

Each employee must be treated as an individual and not categorized as a member of a group. While it is true that different groups (Blacks, Jews, Italians, Indians, etc.) have unique and common customs, this does not mean you should stereotype a member of a race or ethnic group. Each individual thinks, acts and feels differently. Each person has different needs and desires. Each person responds differently to different situations.

Seek and place your trust in individuals who are willing to treat each individual fairly. People have different opinions and positions in life. It is often difficult to determine what is fair and what is not fair. People are fair when they make sound decisions and judgments based on objective reasoning.

Empower Yourself

To obtain success and maintain it we must empower ourselves. Empowerment means believing we are capable of taking responsibility for ourselves and can make a difference in the world. It means actively working to change bad situations, not waiting for someone else to fix them or giving up.

There are things you can do to empower yourself. Accumulate allies to strengthen your position and accomplish your goals. Establish power bases; strong power bases support us in times of prosperity and during times of misfortune. Create them inside and outside your company. They consist of family, friends, employers, co-workers, customers, experts, technology, organizations and leaders that support our goals. You can even find support from enemies when you have common interests.

Always cultivate your power base. Support others so they will support you. Show interest in ideas and projects that are important to others when appropriate. A power base consists of others with common interests. Whenever possible only include supportive members. This does not mean never include people who challenge your ideas. You need objectivity and constructive criticism to make the right decisions. If their concerns are valid, they will save you from failure by identifying problems you can correct.

Having a strong power base makes achieving and maintaining success easier. It also provides financial support and assistance that makes your success possible. It can provide information, guidance, and honest answers.

Strong power bases are deterrents to others who may want to harm you. They are helpful in persuading reluctant parties to support your causes. Strong power bases provide critical moral support when situations become desperate. They are a shoulder to lean on. They allow you the opportunity to express opinions without fear, shame or embarrassment. Use them as sounding boards to try out new ideas. They'll help restore your confidence if you lose it.

Become politically astute and savvy about your environment. Know how to act and what to say. Know when to act and when not to. Know when to speak and when to be quiet. Understand it is not what we say but how we say it. Pick your friends and allies wisely. Know your enemies. Learn to work with individuals you do not like. Develop the skills to turn enemies into allies.

Successful people are masters of office politics. Positioning yourself into a place of power is a never-ending process. It is a process that does not have to be underhanded or sleazy. Provide opportunities that allow everyone to succeed. Acknowledge and reward the contributions of others. Be a mentor to others. Recognize talented individuals and utilize their abilities. In return they will be supportive of your goals.

The Secrets of Success

There is a secret to success that unsuccessful people fail to grasp: *How we share our blessings determines our level of success.* This does not mean giving money or expensive gifts to everyone we meet. That would only make us foolish and poor. It means we must share our time, values, ideas, and financial support when appropriate. It means giving others the respect and rewards they need and the freedom to succeed.

Our actions are meaningful when we provide what others need and not what they *think* they need. We are blessed when we improve the quality of others' lives. What we give must be of value to us and the recipients; otherwise, it is a meaningless gesture. Giving develops meaningful relationships. Showing compassion to the less fortunate without expecting payment enriches our lives.

Studies of successful people show they share common traits. They show success does not happen by chance. Success has little to do with an individual's appearance, size, color, education or religion. In Maxwell Maltz's book, *Psycho-Cybernetics,* he identifies the seven qualities of the success-type personality. Make them an essential part of your character. Memorize and meditate on them daily; they will enrich your life beyond your wildest imagination.

Sense of direction:	Know what you want and where you are going.
Understanding:	Understand what you do and be willing to learn.
Courage:	The ability to face and overcome adversity.
Charity:	A desire and willingness to help others.
Esteem:	Respect yourself and others.
Self confidence:	The conviction to rely on and trust in yourself.
Self acceptance:	Believe in what you do.

Resources

Career Counseling

Going Part-Time:
The Insider's Guide for Professional
Women Who Want a Career and a
Life
Cindy Tolliver and Nancy Chambers
Avon Books, 1997

The Career Discovery Project
Gerald M. Sturman
Main Street Books, 1993

What Color Is Your Parachute?
Richard Bolles Nelson
Ten Speed Press, revised annually.

Job Hunting

Directory of Executive Recruiters
Kennedy Information
One Kennedy Place, Rte. 12S
Fitzwilliam, NH 03447
800 531-0007/603 585-6544

Federal Career Opportunities
Federal Research Services
370 West Maple Avenue
Vienna, VA 22180
(703) 281-0200
Bi-monthly newsletter listing federal
jobs worldwide.

Federal Jobs Digest
325 Pennsylvania Ave., SE
Washington, DC 20003
(914) 762-5111
Bi-monthly newspaper listing federal jobs worldwide.

Forty Plus of Southern California
3450 Wilshire Blvd. Suite 510
Los Angeles, CA 90010
(213) 388-2301
www.fortyplus.org
Non-profit organization assisting job
seekers 40 years and older. Call
information for local chapter.

The Guide to Internet Job Searching
M. Riley Dikel
VGM Career Horizons, 1998

Hook Up, Get Hired:
The Internet.Job Search Revolution
Joyce Lain Kennedy
John Wiley & Sons, 1995.

Job Hunter's Sourcebook
Michelle LeCompte
Gale Research Inc., 1996

National Association of Colleges
and Employers
62 Highland Ave.
Bethlehem, PA 18017
(610)868-1421
(800)544-5257
http://www.jobweb.org/

The National Job Bank
Steven Graber
Adams Media Corp., 1999
Lists more than 21,000 employers by
alphabetically by state; provides
contact and business information.

ProCD Business (CD-ROMs)
List 11 million business numbers,
address, zip codes and SIC codes.
Cost approximately $39.99.
Available in computer stores and by
mail order.

*Standard & Poors Register of
Corporations, Directors, and
Executives*
Three-volume set lists companies by
industry geographically; company
data, personal data on corporate
executives.

Resumé Writing

The Electronic Resumé Revolution
By Joyce Lain Kennedy
John Wiley & Sons, Inc., 1995

**Professional Association of
Resumé Writers**
3637 4th Street, Suite 330
St. Petersburg, FL 33704
(727)821-2274 / (800)822-7927
www.parw.com

Interviewing

*Ask the Headhunter: Reinventing
the Interview to Win the Job*
by Nick Corcodilos
Penguin / Plume,
www.asktheheadhunter.com

*101 Greatest Answers to the
Toughest Interview Questions*
By Ron Fry
Career Press, 1994

Researching Employers

*Billion Dollar Directory: America's
Corporate Families*
Dun & Bradstreet
Lists companies alphabetically, geo-
graphically and by product.

*Thomas Register of American
Manufacturers*
12-volume manufacturing business
directory. A library reference source.

Education and Training

**Distance Education and Training
Council**
1601 18th Street
Washington, DC 20009-2529
(202) 234-5100
Accredits correspondence schools.
Call to verify a distance course is
accredited before enroling.

College Connection
9697 East Mineral Avenue
Englewood, Co 80112
800-777-MIND
Provides distance education access
to more than 30 regionally accredited universities and educational
providers for university degrees.

Maintaining Success

Jump-Start Your Career:
How the "Strengths" that Got You
Where You Are Today Can Hold You
Back Tomorrow
Lois P. Frankel
Three Rivers Press, 1998

Managing with the Power of NLP:
Programming for Personal
Competitive Advantage
David Molden
Financial Times Management, 1996

NLP for Managers: How to Achieve
Excellence at Work
Harry Alder
Piatkus Books, 1998

You Are the Message: Getting What
You Want by Being Who You Are
Roger Ailes
Currency/Doubleday, 1989

Self Employment/ Starting Your Own Business

National Association for the
Self-Employed
P.O. Box 612067
Dallas, TX 75261
(800) 232-6273

National Association for
Home-Based Businesses
P.O. Box 362
10451 Mill Run Circle, #400
Owings Mills, MD 21117
(410)363-3698

Working from Home: Everything You
Need to Know About Living and
Working Under the Same Roof
Paul and Sarah Edwards
Putnam, 1994

Working Solo: The Real Guide to
Freedom and Financial Success with
Your Own Business
Terri Lonier
John Wiley and Sons, 1998
Also available on audio cassette.

Self Publishing

The Complete Guide to Self
Publishing: Everything You Need to
Know to Write, Publish, Promote
and Sell Your Book
(3rd ed.)
Tom Ross and Marilyn Ross
Writers Digest Books, 1994

The Self Publishing Manual:
How to Write, Print and Sell Your
Own Book
(11th ed.)
Dan Poynter
Para Publishing, 1999

Technology

General:

*The Complete Idiot's Guide
to the Internet*
Peter Kent
Que Education and Training, 1998.

Researching Online for Dummies
Reva Basch
IDG Books Worldwide, 1998

*Search Engines for the
World Wide Web*
By Alfred and Emily Glossbrenner
Peachpit Press, 1998

Internet Service Providers (ISPs):

CompuServe
1 800 848-8990

America On-line
1 800 827-6364

Microsoft Network
1 800 386-5550

California Connection
(661) 949-0189
(California residents only)

Web Sites for Employment and Careers

Academic Employment Network
www.academploy.com
Teaching and academic positions

Alta Vista
www.altavista.com
One of the major search engines.
Click on "Careers" to reach a job site
operated by Interim Services
employment agency.

America's Job Bank
www.ajb.dni.us
Lists job openings by state for
employers and job seekers

Bizwomen
www.bizwomen.com
For women who run businesses, or
who would like to.

BridgePath.com
www.bridgepath.com
Specializes in placing new graduates
and alumni. Fill out personal profile
and the site will inform you of available positions that match.

CareerCity
http://www.careercity.com
Lists more than 125,000 job openings, 100 job newsgroups, and links
to 650 corporate employment sites.
Also provides advice, articles.

Career Magazine
www.careermag.com/careermag/
Online magazine providing job
openings, resumé banks, message
board and campus information.

CareerMosaic
www.careermosaic.com
Specialized and general job data
bases; more than 70,000 listings,
updated daily

Career Paradise
www.emory.edu
Job listings for new and recent graduates.

Career Path
www.careerpath.com
300,000 classifieds from more than
65 newspapers (e.g. *Boston Globe,
Chicago Times, New York Times, LA
Times*). Provides searches by category, newspaper, keyword, and date.

Careers & Jobs
www.starthere.com/jobs
Lists every job site available alphabetically and by job type. Provides
information on writing resumés, etc.

FedWorld Information Network
www.fedworld.gov
Federal job data bases updated
daily. Also lists US government Web
sites.

HeadHunter.Net
www.headhunter.net
Provides over 250,000 job listings,
contact names, E-mail addresses,
some phone numbers. You can also
post your resumé here.

HiTechCareers
www.hitechcareer.com

HR Careers Career Center
www.tcm.com/hr-careers
For applicants interested in the
human resources field.

Internet Job Locator
www.joblocator.com
Combines all the major job search
engines on one page. Free access
and posting to resumé data base.

JobDirect
www.jobdirect.com
Cross-references your resumé qualifications with postiions listed by
participating employers, then E-
mails details of each match.

Jobfind.com
www.jobfind.com
Technology job fairs, job searches
and corporate profiles

Jobs.com
www.jobs98.com
Resumé software you can download
and use to upload resumés to a data
base of 800 employers.

Law Employment Center
www.lawjobs.com
Legal profession, positions,
recruiters and law firm job listings.

Monster Board Career Site
www.monster.com
More than 250,000 openings posted.
Resumés also listed.

Petersons.com
www.petersons.com
Comprehensive education resources
on the Web.

Top Jobs USA
www.topjobsusa.com
Only lists professional, managerial
and technical specialist positions.

Other Useful Web Sites:

American City Business Journals
www.amcity.com/
Covers more than 35 weekly business journals from cities across the US.

Ask Jeeves
www.askjeeves.com
A search engine that allows users to type in their questions in plain English.

Business Wire.com
www.hnt.com/bizwire
Online business magazine.

Electronic Newsstand
www.enews.com
Useful for finding articles from a number of popular magazines.

Encyclopedia Britannica Online
www.eb.com/
The premier Web encyclopedia for only $5 a month.

Howard University's Continuing Education
www.con-ed.howard.edu

Small Business Administration
www.sbaonline.sba.gov

Starting Point
www.stpt.com
A Net directory and search tool. you can search by subject or by power search.

Wall Street Journal
www.wsj.com

Resources of Special Interest to Canadians

Alta Vista Canada
www.altavistacanada.com
The Canadian index for this popular search engine.

Canada One
www.canadaone.com
An electronic business magazine for Canadians.

Canada's Best Careers Guide 2000
Frank Feather
Warwick Publishing, Inc.
www.warwickgp.com

Human Resources Development Canada (Job Bank)
http://jb-ge.hrdc-drhc.gc.ca
Job bank run by the Canadian federal government.

References

Business Week, August 10, 1998.

Compuserve Education Forum.

Faulkner, Charles, Gerry Schmidt and Robert McDonald. *NLP:The New Technology of Achievement.* Audio cassette. Nightingale Conant.

Ford, Lisa. *Personal Power.* Audio cassette. CareerTrack Publications.

Frankl, Viktor E. *Man's Search for Meaning.* Washington Square, 1998.

Granovetter, Mark S. *Getting a Job: A Study of Contacts and Careers.* Cambridge: University Press, 1974.

Half, Robert. *How to Get a Better Job in this Crazy World.* Plume Books, 1994.

Kimbro, Dennis and Napoleon Hill. *Think and Grow Rich: A Black Choice.* Fawcett Columbine, 1997.

Maltz, Maxwell. *Psycho-Cybernetics.* Reissue edition. Pocket Books, 1987.

Popcorn, Faith. *The Popcorn Report: Faith Popcorn on the Future of Your Company, Your World, Your Life.* Harper Business, 1992.

Sales & Marketing Management, November 1998, p. 98.

Sharpe, Rochelle. "Losing Ground: In the Latest Recession, Only Blacks Suffered Net Employment Loss," *Wall Street Journal,* September 14, 1993.

Wurman, R. S. *Information Anxiety: What to Doa When Information Doesn't Tell You What You Want or Need to Know.* Bantam Books, 1989.

About the Author

ANTHONY STITH graduated from Rutger's University with a degree in Accounting. He began his professional career as an accountant for KPMG. He went on to work in managerial positions as audit manager and corporate controller for a number of nationally recognized firms.

Mr. Stith is the author of the book *Breaking the Glass Ceiling: Sexism and Racism in Corporate America—the Myths, the Realities and the Solutions*, also available from Warwick Publishing. He has also had articles published in numerous journals.

Mr. Stith is a member of International Black Writers and Artists, the National Writers Association and Toastmaster International. He has appeared as a guest speaker on radio and TV, and has lectured at colleges and universities. He has also been retained as a discrimination expert witness in legal proceedings.

Anthony Stith teaches a variety of workshops on career and employment issues, discrimination, writing, self-help and motivation topics. For more information contact:

Anthony Stith
2763 W. Ave L., PMB 316
Lancaster, CA 93536
USA

Phone/fax (661) 722-8257

E-mail: anthony@anthonystith.com

Web site:
www.anthonystith.com